Excel

YEARS 9 to 10

Grammar and Punctuation Workbook

ESSENTIAL skills

AF585093

Get the Results You Want!

Maya Puiu

© 2015 Maya Puiu and Pascal Press
Reprinted 2019, 2022, 2024

ISBN 978 1 74125 412 9

Pascal Press
PO Box 250
Glebe NSW 2037
(02) 9198 1748
www.pascalpress.com.au

Publisher: Vivienne Joannou
Project editor: Rosemary Peers
Edited by Rosemary Peers
Series developer and consultant: Kristine Brown
Reviewed by Cassandra Freeman
Cover and page design by DiZign Pty Ltd
Typeset by Grizzly Graphics (Leanne Richters)
Printed by Vivar Printing/Green Giant Press

Reproduction and communication for educational purposes
The Australian *Copyright Act 1968* (the Act) allows a maximum of one chapter or 10% of the pages of this work, whichever is the greater, to be reproduced and/or communicated by any educational institution for its educational purposes provided that the educational institution (or the body that administers it) has given a remuneration notice to Copyright Agency under the Act.

For details of the Copyright Agency licence for educational institutions contact:

Copyright Agency
Level 12, 66 Goulburn Street
Sydney NSW 2000
Telephone: (02) 9394 7600
Facsimile: (02) 9394 7601
Email: memberservices@copyright.com.au

Reproduction and communication for other purposes
Except as permitted under the Act (for example, a fair dealing for the purposes of study, research, criticism or review) no part of this book may be reproduced, stored in a retrieval system, communicated or transmitted in any form or by any means without prior written permission. All inquiries should be made to the publisher at the address above.

All efforts to contact individuals regarding copyright have been made and permission acknowledged where applicable. In the event of any oversight, please contact the publisher so correction can be made in subsequent editions.

Contents

To the student

This book has been specifically designed to teach you the essential grammar and punctuation terms, rules and conventions for the Years 9 and 10 Australian Curriculum English course. Knowing more about the grammar of English and about the way we use punctuation will help you develop into a good writer.

Each chapter has two sections: a grammar section and a punctuation section. Each section begins with a sample text and is followed by a boxed explanation of the grammar or punctuation points highlighted in the text.

When you read the explanation, look back to the sample text to understand how the grammar point or rule actually works in written language. The exercises that follow will help you practise your knowledge and apply that knowledge in your own writing.

Each chapter builds on the previous chapter, so when you are working don't be afraid to go back to a previous chapter to revise something you are not sure of.

There are three Revision Tests. The questions in these tests are in the style of NAPLAN Test questions. However, they do not cover every type of question you might get in the NAPLAN Tests. Their purpose is to revise and test the previous five chapters, and so they focus only on the content of these chapters. They will, however, give you practice in the content and structure of many NAPLAN questions.

Always work in good light and take your time. Don't rush, because that's how mistakes happen. With this book and practice, you will know more about the way English works and become a better writer. Good luck!

Maya Puiu

UNIT ONE The Highwayman

Focus

Nouns; commas (1)

Grammar in use

'The Highwayman' by Alfred Noyes

The **wind** was a torrent of darkness among the gusty **trees**,
The **moon** was a ghostly **galleon** tossed upon cloudy **seas**,
The **road** was a ribbon of moonlight over the purple moor,
And the highwayman came riding—
Riding—riding—
The highwayman came riding, up to the old inn-door.

He'd a French cocked-hat on his forehead, a bunch of lace at his chin,
A coat of the claret velvet, and breeches of brown doe-skin;
They fitted with never a wrinkle: his **boots** were up to the thigh!
And he rode with a jewelled twinkle,
His pistol butts a-twinkle,
His rapier hilt a-twinkle, under the jewelled sky.

…

And dark in the dark old inn-yard a stable-wicket creaked
Where **Tim** the ostler listened: his face was white and peaked;
His eyes were hollows of **madness**, his hair like mouldy **hay**,
But he loved the landlord's **daughter**,
The landlord's red-lipped daughter,
Dumb as a dog he listened, and he heard the robber say—

…

About grammar

Nouns name people, places, things, creatures, feelings, ideas and qualities. There are different types of nouns.

- **Common nouns** name people, places or things in general; for example, **trees**, **road**.
- **Proper nouns** name particular or specific people, places or things and always begin with a capital letter; for example, **Alfred**, **Tim**. If the proper noun consists of more than one word, every main word must be capitalised, except for articles, prepositions and conjunctions; for example, *Game of Thrones*.
- **Concrete nouns** are nouns for what can be experienced with the five senses (sight, smell, hearing, taste and touch); for example, **wind**, **moon**, **galleon**, **seas**, **hay**, **daughter**.
- **Abstract nouns** are nouns for what can't be experienced with the five senses, such as feelings or ideas; for example, **madness**. Many abstract nouns are made by turning verbs into nouns (*establish* → *establishment*) and these are called nominalisations. **Nominalisation** is used when writing texts such as essays; it helps to make the action of the sentence more important than the person who is completing the action.
- **Singular nouns** name only one people, place or thing; for example, **road**, **moon**, **daughter**.

- **Plural nouns** name more than one person, place or thing; for example, **trees** and **boots**. Refresh your knowledge of the different rules about making plurals by reviewing the information below.

  For the **plural form** of most nouns, add *s*; for example, **boot → boots**.

  For nouns that end in *ch*, *x*, *s*, or *s* sounds, add *es*; for example, *watch → watches, moss → mosses, bus → buses.*

  For nouns ending in *f* or *fe*, change *f* to *v* and add *es*; for example, *leaf → leaves, life → lives.*

  Some nouns have **irregular plural forms**; for example, *man → men, mouse → mice.*

  For words ending in *y*, if there a vowel before the *y* add *s*; for example, *trolley → trolleys, monkey → monkeys*. If there is a consonant before the *y* change the *y* to *ies*; for example, *lady → ladies, baby → babies.*

  A few nouns have **the same singular and plural forms**; for example, *sheep, deer, series, species.*

  Some nouns are **never plural**; for example, *luggage, furniture* and *information*. They are called **uncountable nouns**.

- The *ing* form of verbs can be used as nouns. These kinds of nouns are called **gerunds**; for example, **Writing** *is an enjoyable activity.* **Reading** *is my favourite pastime.*

  Whether an *ing* word is a noun or verb depends on how it is used in a sentence; for example, *I am* **writing** *poetry*. (verb) **Writing** *is my favourite pastime*. (noun)

  He is always **reading** *poetry*. (verb) **Reading** *helps you learn about the world.* (noun)

- A **noun group** is a group of words that work together around a noun. Through noun groups we can build up a detailed description of the 'things' in our world; for example, we can develop the noun *poem* into *a famous poem* and then into *a very famous poem*, and then *a very famous poem by* **Alfred Noyes**. Many noun groups begin with an **article**; for example, *a, the, an.*

  Noun groups provide more information about the **main noun** in a sentence. The main nouns have been highlighted in the examples below.

  the **highwayman**; **Tim** the ostler; the landlord's red-lipped **daughter**; his pistol **butts**; his rapier **hilt**; a jewelled **twinkle**; a **wrinkle**; a torrent of **darkness**; hollows of **madness**; a French-cocked **hat**; a **coat** of the claret velvet; the old **inn-door**; the jewelled **sky**

Boost your grammar skills

1 Review your knowledge of nouns by underlining every **common noun** and circling every **proper noun** in the following extract.

> He did not come in the dawning; he did not come at noon;
> And out of the tawny sunset, before the rise of the moon,
> When the road was a gypsy's ribbon, looping the purple moor,
> A red-coat troop came marching—
> Marching—marching—
> King George's men came marching, up to the old inn-door.

2 Write the following **nouns** in the correct spaces. The first one has been done for you.

England authorities poem revenge Bess success Alfred Noyes death ambush

'The Highwayman' is a narrative ___poem___ written by ________________, first published in 1906. The following year it was included in Noyes's collection, *Forty Singing Seamen and Other Poems*, becoming an immediate ________________. The poem, set in 18th-century rural ________________, tells the story of an unnamed highwayman who is in love with ________________, a landlord's daughter. Betrayed to the ________________ by Tim, a jealous ostler, the highwayman escapes ________________ when Bess sacrifices her life to warn him. Learning of her ________________, he dies in a futile attempt at ________________, shot down on the highway. In the final stanza, the ghosts of the lovers meet again on winter nights.

Adapted from https://en.wikipedia.org/wiki/The_Highwayman_(poem)

3 Underline the **abstract nouns** in the following sentences.

For example: The creation of a stormy setting establishes the dark tone of the poem.

a On one level, the poem is a description of a windy night and the highwayman's approach on horseback.

b There is a strong connection with stormy waters, as seen in 'a torrent of darkness' and 'cloudy seas'.

c The poet's creation of the world seems oddly unsettled and even the moon itself seems unstable—it is 'tossed' about in the sky.

d Instrumental to the poem is the association of the highwayman with the chaotic and mysterious forces of nature.

4 To the following singular nouns, add an *s* or *es* to form their **plurals**. Some words will remain unchanged as their plural form is the same as their singular, or because they only have a singular form.

a stable-wicket ________________

b shutter ________________

c blood ________________

d sky ________________

e sweat ________________

f madness ________________

g hay ________________

h moonlight ________________

i curse ________________

j darkness ________________

k kiss ________________

l foot ________________

m dark ________________

n hoof ________________

o breath ________________

5 Next to the following sentences, write *N* or *V* to identify whether the underlined *ing* word is used as a **noun** (a gerund) or as part of the **verb**.

a A painting of *The Highwayman* is in the national gallery. ________________

b I'm enjoying tonight's poetry reading. ________________

c The poem 'The Highwayman' has a fantastic ending. ________________

d The meeting of the two lovers was doomed from the start. ________________

e The 'ghostly galleon' was tossing over the night sky. ________________

f Bess was waiting for the highwayman's return. ________________

6 In each of the following **noun groups** underline the **main noun** by asking the question 'What?' For example, in the first question, in *his whip on the shutters*, asking 'What was on the shutters?' will locate the main noun *whip*.

a his whip on the shutters
b the yellow gold before the morning light
c the black cascade of perfume
d its waves in the moonlight
e the tawny sunset
f the rise of the moon
g the stroke of midnight

Punctuation in use

Poetry has a long history, dating back to the Sumerian *Epic of Gilgamesh*. **Ancient attempts to define poetry, such as Aristotle's *Poetics*, focused on the uses of speech in rhetoric, drama, song and comedy. More modern attempts concentrated on features such as repetition, verse form and rhyme, and focused more on the feelings being communicated.**
Adapted from https://en.wikipedia.org/wiki/Poetry

About punctuation

- **Commas** help us make our meaning clear by separating the different parts of a sentence. One use is to **separate items** in a list of three or more; for example, **Ancient attempts to define poetry, such as Aristotle's *Poetics*, focused on the uses of speech in rhetoric, drama, song and comedy**.
- We don't usually place a comma after **the second-last item in a list** (before *and* or *or*). However, a comma may be used this way where the items in the list include **two or more words**, or where the sentence is long; for example, **More modern attempts concentrated on features such as repetition, verse form and rhyme, and focused more on the feelings being communicated**.
- As a general guide, commas may be used where we feel they are needed so that a sentence **makes sense**. Reading a sentence aloud is a technique that will help you decide where to place commas; you should place a comma where there are **natural pauses** in your speech.

Boost your punctuation skills

1 Add **commas** where necessary in the following sentences.

a A melodic effect can be achieved from poetic techniques such as assonance alliteration onomatopoeia and rhythm.
b In our modern society a variety of cultures and languages influence poetic forms styles and techniques.
c Visual images word association and a language's musical qualities influence how a poem is created.
d Different types of meter played key roles in Classical Early European Eastern and Modern poetry.
e The line couplet stanza and verse paragraph form the main elements of a poem's structure.

2 The following information contains too many **commas**. Cross out the unnecessary commas.

The development, of auditory skills comes from listening to poems, and songs. While you read, sing, play, and act out poems you are learning that, sounds make words and that words can be fun, amusing, and enjoyable.

3 Tick the correct answer in the following sentence pairs.

a ☐ Reading poetry offers joy excitement and insight to both new and inexperienced readers.

☐ Reading poetry offers joy, excitement and insight to both new and inexperienced readers.

b ☐ The act of creating poetry strengthens individuals, including realisations about who you are what you think, what your life has been like, what you want and what you want to accomplish.

☐ The act of creating poetry strengthens individuals, including realisations about who you are, what you think, what your life has been like, what you want, and what you want to accomplish.

c ☐ People write poetry through a desire to, share, promote education or be inspirational

☐ People write poetry through a desire to share, promote education, or be inspirational.

d ☐ Poetry can be publicly recognised by sharing, reading, posting or publishing.

☐ Poetry can be publicly recognised by sharing, reading, posting, or publishing.

e ☐ People who write poetry may become more sensitive to larger issues in life, feel connected, and develop an appreciation of life.

☐ People who write poetry may become more sensitive to larger issues in life feel connected and develop an appreciation of life.

4 In the following famous quotes by poets add the missing **commas.** Reading the sentences aloud will help you with meaning and comma placement.

a 'Poetry is what in a poem makes you laugh cry prickle be silent makes your toe nails twinkle makes you want to do this or that or nothing makes you know that you are alone in the unknown world.' Dylan Thomas

b 'The poet's mind is in fact a receptacle for seizing and storing up numberless feelings phrases and images which remain there until all the particles which can unite to form a new compound are present together.' T S Eliot

c 'There are three things that a poem must reach: the eye the ear and what we may call the heart or the mind. It is most important of all to reach the heart of the reader.' Robert Frost

d 'Use no superfluous word no adjective which does not reveal something.' Ezra Pound

e 'Poetry is simply the most beautiful impressive and widely effective mode of saying things and hence its importance.' Matthew Arnold

UNIT TWO

Jane Eyre

Focus

Pronouns; commas (2)

Grammar in use

From *Jane Eyre* by Charlotte Bronte

Mrs Reed's hands still lay on **her** work inactive: **her** eye of ice continued to dwell freezingly on mine.

'**What** more have you to say?' **she** asked, rather in the tone in which a person might address an opponent of adult age than such as is ordinarily used to a child.

That eye of **hers**, that voice stirred every antipathy **I** had. Shaking from head to foot, thrilled with ungovernable excitement, I continued '**I** am glad **you** are no relation of **mine**: I will never call **you** aunt again as long as I live. I will never come to see you when I am grown up; and if anyone asks me how I liked you, and how you treated **me**, I will say the very thought of you makes me sick, and that you treated me with miserable cruelty.'

About grammar

Pronouns are words that replace nouns. They are helpful as they allow us to avoid repeating the nouns we are referring to. For example, *Mrs Reed* is referred to with the pronouns *hers, she* and *you*. Some of the main types of pronouns are shown below:

- **Personal pronouns** are used to refer to yourself, the people you are talking to, or the people or things you are talking about. The novel *Jane Eyre* is written from the perspective of the character Jane Eyre. She refers to herself using the first-person pronoun *I*.
  Personal pronouns can be:
  - **subject pronouns**—*I, we, you, he,* **she**, *it* or *they*; for example, **I** *am glad* (*I* is the subject of the sentence)
  - **object pronouns**—*me, us,* **you**, *him, her, it* or *them*; for example, *you treated* **me** (*me* is the object of the sentence).
- **Possessive pronouns** are used to show ownership. The possessive pronouns are *mine, yours, his, hers, ours* and theirs; for example, *you are no relation of* **mine**, *That eye of* **hers**.
  Possessive adjectives are also used to show ownership. For example, *her* is a possessive adjective replacing *Mrs Reed's* in the sentence *Mrs Reed's hands still lay on* **her** *work inactive:* **her** *eye of ice*. Other possessive adjectives are *my, your, his, her, its, our* and *their; for example,* **my** *book,* **her** *aunt,* **our** *childhood*. These adjectives are sometimes referred to as possessive pronouns so they are covered in this chapter. While possessive pronouns are able to stand on their own in a sentence, possessive adjectives need to be associated with another noun to make sense: possessive pronouns are used to **replace** the noun but possessive adjectives are used to **describe** a noun so they always go before a noun or noun phrase.
- **Interrogative pronouns** are used to ask questions. There are four main interrogative pronouns: *who* or *whom, what, which* and *whose*. Mrs Reed uses an interrogative pronoun when she says **What** *more have you to say? Whom* is the correct form when the pronoun is the object of the verb, as in **Whom** *did Jane see?* (*Jane saw John*). However, *whom* is used less and less these days in everyday communication.

- **Demonstrative pronouns** are the words *this, that, these* and *those* used as pronouns. *This* and *these* generally (but not always) refer to something **close**; for example, *Is* **this** *Jane Eyre?/Have you* **read** *these? That* and *those* generally refer to something **further away**; for example, **Those** *on the top shelf are children's books.*/**That** *is my favourite.*
- All pronouns must **agree in number and gender** with the noun they replace (either singular or plural); for example, **Eliza, John** *and* **Georgiana were** *now clustered round* **their** *mama in the drawing-room* **not** 'Eliza, **John** and **Georgiana was** now clustered round **her** mama in the drawing-room.'

Boost your grammar skills

1 Circle the **main noun** in the following sentences, and then underline its corresponding pronoun.

For example: (Jane Eyre) has, from the very start, a sense of self-respect and confidence. <u>She</u> shows a personal obligation to honesty and high standards.

a 'Wicked and cruel boy!' I said. 'You are like a murderer—you are like a slave-driver—you are like the Roman emperors!'

b 'I feared nothing but interruption, and that came too soon.'

c 'No; moonlight was still, and this stirred; while I gazed.'

d Whom did she blame for the family's hostility? John Reed?

2 Write an appropriate **pronoun** or **possessive adjective** in the spaces.

> Born on 21 April 1816, in Thornton, Yorkshire, England, Charlotte Brontë worked as a teacher and governess before collaborating on a book of poetry with ________ two sisters, Emily and Anne, who were writers as well. In 1847, ________ published the semi-autobiographical novel *Jane Eyre*, which was a hit and would become a literary classic. ________ other novels included *Shirley* and *Villette*. ________ died on 31 March 1855, in Haworth, Yorkshire, England. *Jane Eyre* creates a strong impact on the reader. ________ provides ________ with a detailed narration of events, realistic dialogue, as well as revealing Jane's inner thoughts and feelings.

3 Insert one of the following **pronouns** into each of the following sentences from *Jane Eyre*. Remember: pronouns must agree with their corresponding nouns. Next to each sentence, write *S* if you have used a subject pronoun, or *O* if you have used an object pronoun.

He	you	I	he	him	me	you	us

For example: 'Boh! Madam Mope!' cried the voice of John Reed; then __he__ paused: he found the room apparently empty. __S__

a 'You be seated somewhere; and until ______ can speak pleasantly, remain silent.' ______

b 'And I came out immediately, for ______ trembled at the idea of being dragged forth by the said Jack.' ______

c John Reed was a schoolboy of 14 years old; four years older than I, for I was but 10: ______ gorged himself habitually at table, which made ______ bilious, and gave him a dim and bleared eye and flabby cheeks. ______ and ______

d He bullied and punished ______; not two or three times in the week, nor once or twice in the day, but continually: every nerve I had feared him, and every morsel of flesh in my bones shrank when he came near. ______

e 'You have no business to take our books; ______ are a dependant, Mama says; you have no money; your father left you none; you ought to beg, and not to live here with gentlemen's children like ______.' ______ and ______

4 Write the missing **possessive pronoun** or **possessive adjective** using the space clues.

a *Jane Eyre* is about the life of a young girl called Jane Eyre. It is ____________ story.

b Jane said that Mrs Reed was no relation of ____________.

c John Reed threw his book at ____________ cousin Jane.

d Jane resides with ____________ cousins at Gateshead Hall. She is made to feel unwanted, however, and everything in the house is ____________, not ____________ .

e *Jane Eyre* influences ____________ understanding of what life was like in England during the mid-1800s.

5 Use the correct **interrogative pronoun** in the following questions and answers.

a __________ is the name of the book? *Jane Eyre* is the name of the book.

b __________ is Jane Eyre? The main character of the story

c __________ wrote *Jane Eyre?* Charlotte Bronte

d To __________ is Jane talking in the extract? Her aunt, Mrs Reed

e __________ eyes dwell 'freezingly' on Jane's? Mrs Reed's

f __________ person is Jane antagonised by? John Reed, Jane's cousin

Other types of pronouns

Pronouns are extremely important little words. Without them we would find it difficult to connect ideas within and between sentences. Here are some other types of common pronouns.

* **Indefinite pronouns** are words that do not refer to any particular person, amount, or thing; for example, *anything, something, anyone* and *everyone*. The indefinite pronoun must agree in both **number** and **gender** with the words it refers to; for example, **Many** *have expressed* **their** *views on the novel./ I will do* **anything** *to solve the problem, even if* **it** *takes me all year.*

  Singular indefinite pronouns include *another, anybody, anyone, anything, each, either, everybody, everyone, everything, neither, nobody, no one, nothing, one, other, somebody, someone* and *something.*

  Plural indefinite pronouns include *both, few, many, others* and *several.*

  Some indefinite pronouns can be **either singular or plural** depending on the sentence. These include *all, any, none* and *most.*

  Note: there is sometimes an **agreement** issue with indefinite pronouns. Some would say that the sentence **Everyone** *wanted to read* **their** *books* is grammatically incorrect, as *everyone* is singular and *their* is plural. They would say that it should be **Everyone** *wanted to read* **his or her** *book*. However, the first form is now quite acceptable in most contexts of speech and writing, because the second form can sound rather awkward. A way around the problem is to reword and use a plural pronoun instead. That is, it may be simpler to say **They all** *wanted to read* **their** *books.*

Another issue is that keeping singular agreement sometimes leads to a choice of one gender only, often male; for example, **Everyone** *wanted to read* **his** *book*. Unless *everyone* was male, this would generally be considered gender-biased language.

- **Reflexive pronouns** are used when you want to show that the object of a verb is the same person or thing as the subject of the verb; for example, in the sentence *Jane wrapped herself in a shawl*, Jane did the wrapping and she was also the person who the shawl was wrapped around.

  Singular reflexive pronouns are *myself, yourself, himself, herself* and *itself.*

  Plural reflexive pronouns are *ourselves, yourselves* and *themselves.*

  Note: avoid the common errors of 'hisself' and 'theirselves'. These are **not** correct forms.

- **Reciprocal pronouns** are the expressions *each other* and *one another* which indicate that people do the same thing and feel the same way; for example, *Jane and John dislike* **each other** or *They dislike* **one another**. There is very little difference between *each other* and *one another*. When *each* and *other* are separated in the sentence, a singular verb is always used after *each*; for example, **Each is** *in the debt of the* **other**.

6 Underline the **correct verb** or **pronoun** to make each sentence correct:

a I can't decide which main character I like the best as both (is/are) so enjoyable to read about.

b The Bronte sisters wrote many books. Several (are/is) considered classics.

c Each of the two girls (is/are) determined to achieve more than the (other/others).

d I saw two modern film versions of the film. Neither (have/has) excited me with (its/their) originality.

e This book has a wide audience. Everyone (is/are) able to access (them/it).

7 Correct this student's English report for **pronoun use** and for **pronoun/verb agreement**. Remember: each pronoun must agree in both **number** and **gender**.

> Few is able to disagree that *Jane Eyre* is a classic novel. The story begin with Jane as a girl alone but with a defiant spirit. It slowly changes into an intelligent young woman who is fiercely independent. Throughout her story, Jane are met with hostility from those around it, often because of problems resulting from low social class. However, when Jane meets Rochester, both are immediately attracted to the other. Everyone are opposed to the match, yet Jane maintain her independent spirit.

Punctuation in use

The role and standing of women in the Victorian era is a significant theme in Charlotte Brontë's *Jane Eyre*. **As a young woman, petite and of relatively low social standing, Jane encounters men during her journey who are of morally debatable character**. It takes great personal strength to overcome the influence of other characters. A perfect example is Mr Rochester who, despite claiming to love Jane unselfishly, is more often observed speaking to her in an authoritative manner; for example, **'Come to my side, Jane, and let us explain and understand one another.' Jane, conversely, believes in the importance of women's independence**, and makes her own decisions throughout the novel.

About punctuation

Commas are often used to separate from the rest of the sentence:

- **extra information** about a noun—information that might be interesting but which can be taken out without affecting the meaning of the sentence; for example, *As a young woman,* **petite and of relatively low social standing***, Jane encounters men during her journey who are of morally debatable character.*
- **connecting words and expressions** like *however, nevertheless, in fact, similarly* and *conversely.* These may occur at the beginning of a sentence; for example, **However***, many of them attempt to establish,* or in the middle of the sentence; for example, *Jane,* **conversely***, believes in the importance of women's independence.*
- **names of people** within sentences; for example, *'Come to my side,* **Jane***, and let us explain and understand one another.'*

Boost your punctuation skills

1 Add the missing **commas**.

- **a** The only time Jane the book's protagonist truly feels ready to make a decision is after she has consulted her own personal moral compass.
- **b** In addition Mr Rochester becomes lame and blind after the fire that ripped through his home.
- **c** 'Don't be afraid Jane I saw it was an accident.'
- **d** The novel however also discloses that Brontë considered Victorian society patriarchal.
- **e** While the dominant characters present in Jane's life throughout the novel all try in a variety of ways to control her she is largely resistant.
- **f** 'How dare you affirm that Jane Eyre?'

2 Cross out the mistakes and add **commas** where necessary in these sentences. Reading the sentences out loud will help you decide where there are natural pauses in the sentences.

- **a** The main journey, in *Jane Eyre* is Jane's search for love, for feelings of belonging and family.
- **b** Nevertheless Jane's quest is continually strengthened, by her desire for freedom.
- **c** We meet her as an orphan, who is preoccupied with wanting to reinforce her worth, and realise happiness.

d While, she does not receive any real love from Mrs Reed Jane does find other women to form relationships with, in the novel.

e In the novel men such, as Mr Rochester her Uncle John and St John are able easily to make decisions for themselves.

3 Mark the incorrectly punctuated sentences with a cross (✗), then rewrite them with the correct punctuation on the lines below.

Remember the **comma** rules from the previous chapter. Reading the sentences out loud will help you decide where there are natural pauses in the sentences.

a Jane's future is influenced by her lack of social advantage, fortune and good looks, and she is disadvantaged as a result of this.

b Jane refers to herself as 'poor, obscure, plain and little', reminding the reader of the young and lonely child she was.

c However in not following a path of conformity, Jane challenges convention and this does reveal the distinctive features of a heroine.

d Primarily, Jane Eyre is a young woman who faces difficulties with purpose and strength of character. Brought up by Mrs Reed, a hard woman, she is sent to Lowood, a dreary charity school run by the authoritarian Mr Brocklehurst, where she attempts to rise above her situation.

e *Jane Eyre* is often referred to as the earliest notable feminist novel, although in the book there are no themes relating to political, legal, educational, or intellectual equality between the sexes.

4 The following passage needs **commas**. Use all your knowledge to place **commas** where necessary.

> Jane's independence continues to show through. She does not enjoy Rochester smothering her in money clothes and attention. She is in fact fearful that they will change her personal values and morals. She tries to resist. 'I would as soon see you Mr Rochester tricked out in stage-trappings as myself clad in a court-lady's robe.' Furthermore Jane declares that until she is married to Mr Rochester she will continue to be Adèle's governess and earn her usual wage. This information which may surprise some readers further demonstrates Jane's desire to prioritise her independence.

UNIT THREE

A cycling experience

Focus

Verbs; commas (3)

Grammar in use

Keiichi Iwasaki **is** a 36-year-old Japanese tourist who **has spent** eight years cycling more than 45 000 km across 37 countries with the equivalent of just $2 in his pocket, and who **is relying** on his bicycle for transport.

Initially, Iwasaki **left** his home for a short tour through Japan. He **liked** the trip so much that he extended his trip and **hitched** a ride on a ferry to South Korea and began **to travel** the world. 'Most travellers and adventurers dislike cycling for long periods and need money, but instead of giving up I take every opportunity **to explore** the world. **Having experienced** a lot, I want to clarify that dreams can come true if you are willing to take risks,' Iwasaki said.

Despite his best intentions, Iwasaki ran into trouble on many occasions. He **was robbed** by pirates, attacked in Tibet by a rabid dog, **escaped** marriage in Nepal and **was arrested** in India. He **is** not certain yet when he **will return** home.

Adapted from
http://en.wikinews.org/wiki/Japanese_tourist_travels_through_37_countries_on_just_$2

About grammar

- **Verbs** are important as they tell us what is occurring in a sentence.
- **Verbs** express a **physical action**, a **mental action** or a **relationship**; for example, *Iwasaki* **left** *his home* (physical action), *He* **liked** *the trip* (mental action), *He* **is** *not certain* (relationship).
- Some **verbs** are known as **helping** (or **auxiliary**) verbs; for example, *Iwasaki …* **has** *spent eight years cycling,* and *He* **was robbed** *by pirates.* Common **auxiliary verbs** include *is, are, was, were, do, did, does, will, have, has, had, can, may, might, should, could* and *would.*
- **Verbs** change form to different **tenses** to show when things happen. The **present tense** shows what is happening now; for example, *Iwasaki* **is** *a 36-year-old.* The **past tense** tells about events in the past; for example, *[he]* **escaped** *marriage in Nepal.* The **future tense** tells about the future; for example, *he* **will** *return home.*
- We show **continuous action** with auxiliary verbs and the *ing* form of the verb; for example, *[he]* **is relying** *on his bicycle for transport.* Continuous action can be used in all tenses (*was relying, is relying, will be relying*).
- When a verb is made of more than one word it is called a **verb group**. When you form a verb group, you use a combination of **auxiliary verbs** and **participles**.
- **Participles** are **partial verb forms**. The **present participle** is the *ing* verb form; for example, *Iwasaki …* **is relying** *on his bicycle.* The **past participle** is usually the *ed* form of the verb; for example, *For eight years Iwasaki has* **relied** *on his bicycle.* Sometimes, however, the past participle is irregular; for example, *[he]* **has spent** *eight years cycling.*

- Verb groups can be in the **active** or **passive voice**. You use the **active voice** to focus on the performer of an action, such as *he* **liked** *the trip so much* and *when he* **will return** *home*. You use the **passive voice** to focus on the action itself, or the person or thing being acted upon; for example, *He* **was robbed** *by pirates ...* **was arrested** *in India*. (Active and passive forms of the verb are the focus of Unit 9.)
- Verbs are either **finite** (complete) or **non-finite** (incomplete).
- A **finite verb** is a verb which has a subject and shows tense; for example, *Iwasaki ...* **hitched** *a ride on a ferry. Iwasaki* is the verb's subject and the verb *hitched* tells us the event occurred in the **past**. Every sentence must have a finite verb.
- A **non-finite verb** is a verb that is not complete and which cannot stand alone to make a sentence. *Hitching a ride on a ferry ...* or *To hitch a ride on a ferry ...* are not sentences as they only contain non-finite verbs.
- There are two types of non-finite verbs: **infinitives** (verbs containing the word *to*); for example, **to travel** *the world*, **to explore** *the world;* and **participles** (mostly *ing* and *ed* verbs); for example, **Having experienced** *a lot* and **robbed** *by pirates.*
- Verbs must always **agree in number** with their nouns; for example, *Bikes have two wheels* not 'Bikes has two wheels', and **Cyclists**, *travelling locally or not, are required to maintain their bike for safety purposes* not '**Cyclists**, travelling locally or not, is required to maintain their bike for safety purposes.'

Boost your grammar skills

1 Underline the **verb** or verbs in each sentence. They may be a single verb or a verb group.

- **a** My bike has created obvious health benefits for this 60-year-old.
- **b** I was knocked off my bike by a driver in a Porsche last July.
- **c** I went on longer and longer rides until someone suggested that I needed a more appropriate bike for such distances.
- **d** My sister recommended the bike as she knew I would find it a great tension release.
- **e** I would cycle to work if I could, and if it was not dangerous
- **f** The idea that we could evolve into a society that loves bicycles is one that pleases me immensely.

2 Circle the appropriate **helping (auxiliary) verb** in the gaps to complete the verb groups.

- **a** He (had/have) left home for a short tour before deciding to travel the world.
- **b** He (will/would) like to continue travelling but (may/does) choose instead to return home.
- **c** He (do/does) not want to let his bad experiences ruin his adventure.
- **d** He (should/can) (have/has) saved some more money before leaving.
- **e** He (had/will) create many lasting memories of his experiences and the people he's met.

3 Identify each of the following underlined verb groups as either *P* for passive voice or *A* for active voice.

- **a** She enjoyed cycling during the cooler winter months. ______
- **b** The mayor wanted to make it clear that cycling lanes would be introduced. ______
- **c** Local farmers have allowed the cyclists to ride through their land. ______
- **d** She was given the bike as a birthday present and has enjoyed it immensely. ______
- **e** When the rain started, they were taken to a local hall for rest and refreshments. ______

4 In the following examples, tick (✔) only those that contain **finite verbs** and which are therefore correct sentences.

a To ride on the left-hand side of the road. ______

b Riding with broken brakes carries a hefty fine. ______

c Having received a maximum penalty of five years in prison and a hefty fine. ______

d Having cycled to work. ______

e All bikes are required to have a bell. ______

f Including many chances to win a bike. ______

5 Circle the correct form of the **verb** (singular or plural) in each sentence.

a The rhythm created by long-distance cycling (is/are) soothing.

b I hope you, while on your amazing trip, (remember/remembers) to write to me regularly.

c Hardest hit by the summer temperatures (was/were) the long-distance cyclists.

d My cycling friends and my school friends (like/likes) each other tremendously.

e The number of cyclists on the road (is/are) increasing every year.

6 Rewrite the following information to correct the **tense** inconsistencies and lack of **agreement**.

> **Why cycle Japan?** Japan is a beautiful country to explore by bicycle. The countryside was sparsely populated with little traffic, but still offered a strong cycling infrastructure. There are numerous unexpected country back road, and many of those were tarsealed and comfortable to ride. Japanese drivers was very courteous. The diversity of food, culture, history and natural environment is so interesting that most people will have returned to Japan.

____

____

____

____

Perfect-tense verbs

- The **perfect tense** is a tense created with a form of **have** and a **past participle**; for example, *Iwasaki* **has spent** *eight years cycling; he* **had been** *cycling for some time.* The perfect tense allows us to speak and write more accurately about when things happened and in what order.
- The **present perfect** tense is used to talk about past events that still have a connection to the present, using the present tense form of *have* and a past participle; for example, *He* **has escaped** *marriage in Nepal.*
- The **past perfect** tense refers to past events which happened earlier than other past tense events using the past tense form of *have* and a past participle; for example, *He* **had escaped** *marriage in Nepal.*
- The **future perfect** tense can be used to refer to something that has not happened yet, but will happen before a particular time in the future; for example, *By the time he returns home, he* **will have** *escaped marriage in Nepal.*
- The perfect tense is also possible in **continuous** forms. It uses the *ing* form of the verb to show something that started in the past and continues in the present; for example, *He* **has been riding** *all his life* and *He* **has been training** *for hours.*

7 Underline the correct **perfect tense** in the following questions.

- **a** When I met Iwasaki he (had been/has been) cycling for a long time
- **b** How long (has Iwasaki been cycling/had Iwasaki been cycling) when I first met him?
- **c** Iwasaki (has spent/had spent) eight years cycling since he turned 36.
- **d** Before we were acquainted, I (had seen/had been seeing) Iwasaki only once.
- **e** Iwasaki promised me he (has/will have) his bike serviced by the end of next week.

8 Convert each word in brackets to the appropriate **tense** form to complete this passage.

I (see) ______________ many interesting things during my journey through Japan. I (climb) ______________ a mountain with my bike on my back. By the time I returned home, I (experience) ______________ ______________ more than most people my age.

When I finally (see) ______________ my mother after eight years, her eyes were red and teary. I think she may (cry) ______________ ______________ ______________.

Tomorrow, I (begin) ______________ ______________ to record some of my experiences. Just to be safe, I (save) ______________ ______________ ______________ my work often so I don't lose it!

Punctuation in use

Interviewer: When did what you'd achieved sink in?

Iwasaki: It hasn't yet. Maybe it's starting to this week.

Interviewer: **You know**, I'm surprised. Why is it not sinking in?

Iwasaki: When you ride for that long, with so little, you're so focused on surviving. It's life and death stuff, **isn't it**?

Interviewer: Is that why you feel so mentally tired?

Iwasaki: The journey itself demanded a lot of concentration and focus, so that is one of the most fatiguing features of the experience, **I believe**.

About punctuation

Commas are often used to separate:

- **short expressions** like *wow, um, gosh, you know* and *please* from the rest of the sentence; for example, **You know**, *I'm surprised.*
- **question tags** such as *will you* or *isn't it*; for example, *It's life and death stuff,* **isn't it***?*
- **ending comments** from the rest of the sentence, such as *I think, I suppose, I suggest, I wonder*; for example, *so that is one of the most fatiguing features of the experience,* **I believe**.

Commas are used in a variety of ways and always have the purpose of **making meaning clearer**.

Boost your punctuation skills

1 Put commas around **short expressions** or **question tags** in the following sentences.

- **a** Hey I wanted to tell you about what happened during my trip.
- **b** He's had an amazing journey hasn't he?
- **c** Goodness gracious nearly getting married was the event that most scared me!
- **d** You know I would love to hear more about your trip.
- **e** You won't be staying long in India will you?

2 This text contains seven **commas**. Circle the three commas that should not be there.

> Hi, my name is Keiichi, Iwasaki. I am a Japanese man who is travelling around the world. You might see me riding past on my bike, or working as a street performer. I need to entertain people to earn a living. My travel started, I think, about nine years ago. Through this journey I would like to learn how we can make the world, a better place. Support me, please!

3 Tick (✔) the sentences that use **commas** correctly. Rewrite those that don't.

- **a** Gourmet Cycling Travel leads a six-day journey through Provence with stops for wine, chocolate tastings, local market visits, and private château cooking classes.
- **b** I would mostly consider myself a rock climber and I love being in the mountains. When my friend asked if I would like to bicycle from the Pacific to the Atlantic, I said yes, without hesitation.
- **c** I mean really how hard could the ride be right? It ended up being pretty hard. I got sick during the first week and woke up every night with a hacking cough for 10 days.
- **d** Lastly you become a machine. You are a pair of legs a pair of lungs, and a stomach that never fills.

4 Add the missing **commas** to these sentences. You should use your knowledge about commas from previous chapters.

- **a** I was worried when the instructor said 'Come here Alina' but she just wanted to remind me about the competition.
- **b** When beginning training you should warm up do a mixed-intensity workout and then cool down.
- **c** Stop every 10 to 20 kilometres depending on your ability. Consume some water eat some food and check your bike for any problems.
- **d** Warm up and stretch for 10 minutes. Star jumps jogging on the spot and various leg stretches work best. This will avoid cramps in the legs especially thighs.
- **e** Generally speaking beginning with a short ride even around the block will get you started.

5 Improve the following email by placing **commas** where necessary.

> How to pack for such a trip Henry? I suggest that since we will also be taking the train we should not bring bike luggage spare parts or load ourselves down. Do you know anyone else who has done a biking trip like this in Japan and if so could you ask them for some recommendations? I am inclined to pack my normal rolling suitcase adapt to bike travel as needed and see how we go. We will certainly come equipped with raincoats rain pants and wet weather gear. I mean we're used to doing that at home! It's going to be tricky isn't it?

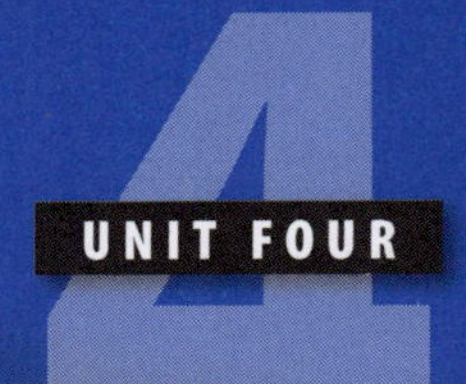

UNIT FOUR

Animal Farm

Focus

Verbs (2); commas (4)

Grammar in use

From *Animal Farm* by George Orwell

Animal Farm *was published towards the end of World War II, in England in 1945. George Orwell wrote the book as a cautionary allegory, which is an extended metaphor. This was designed to send society a warning about the dangers presented by Russian leader Joseph Stalin and similar totalitarian governments. Orwell uses animal characters, such as pigs, dogs and horses to represent historical characters and events so that the reader can understand ideas more clearly.*

Mr Jones, of the Manor Farm, **had locked** the hen-houses for the night, but **was** too drunk to remember to shut the pop-holes. With the ring of light from his lantern dancing from side to side, he **lurched** across the yard, **kicked** off his boots at the back door, **drew** himself a last glass of beer from the barrel in the scullery, and **made** his way up to bed, where Mrs Jones was already snoring.

As soon as the light in the bedroom **went** out there was a stirring and a fluttering all through the farm buildings. Word had **gone** round during the day that old Major, **the prize Middle White boar**, had had a strange dream on the previous night and wished to communicate it to the other animals.

About grammar

Irregular verbs

- The **past tense** of a verb usually consists of the **base verb** with *ed* on the end; for example, *he lurch***ed**, *he kick***ed**. These verbs are known as **regular verbs**.
- The **past participle** of regular verbs is also formed by adding *ed*; for example, *he locked* (past tense) *he* **had locked** (auxiliary verb *had* and past participle *locked*).
- **Irregular verbs** change form completely in the past tense and past participle. Sometimes the form is the same for both. For example, both the past tense and the past participle of the verb *make* is *made*: *He made* (past tense) and *he has made* (auxiliary and past participle).
- Irregular verbs can be **confusing** and verbs like *lay* and *lie* are often mixed up. One way of knowing which one to use is to remember that **you lay something** down but people **lie down by themselves**; for example, *George Orwell* **lays** *his book on the table and* **lies** *on his bed.* Another set of confusing verbs is *bought* and *brought*. *Bought* is the past tense of the verb *buy*, while *brought* is the past tense of the verb *bring*; for example, *I* **bought** *Animal Farm from the bookshop and have* **brought** *it to your house to show you.*
- However, with many **irregular verbs** the **past tense** and the **past participle** of the verb are **different**. For example, the past tense of the base verb *go* is **went**, while its past participle is **gone**. The following list contains 19 common irregular verbs.

Base verb	Past tense	Past participle	Base verb	Past tense	Past participle
be	was	been	give	gave	given
bring	brought	brought	lay	laid	laid
buy	bought	bought	lie	lay	lain
catch	caught	caught	lose	lost	lost
choose	chose	chosen	ring	rang	rung
come	came	come	see	saw	seen
creep	crept	crept	take	took	taken
do	did	done	tear	tore	torn
draw	drew	drawn	wake	woke	woken
drink	drank	drunk			

Boost your grammar skills

1 Fill in the correct **past tense verb** or **past participle verb** in the following sentences.

For example: First (come) ___came___ the three dogs, Bluebell, Jessie and Pincher, and then the pigs.

a God had (give) ______________ him a tail to keep the flies off.

b Four large rats had (creep) ______________ out of their holes.

c It had (be) ______________ agreed that they should all meet in the big barn as soon as Mr Jones (be) ______________ safely out of the way.

d The dogs had suddenly (catch) ______________ sight of them, and it was only by a swift dash for their holes that the rats saved their lives.

e The two horses had (lie) ______________ on the straw for two days when a brood of ducklings, which had (lost) ______________ their mother, filed into the barn.

2 Fill in the chart with the correct **past tense verbs** and **past participle verbs**. You may need to use a dictionary if you are not sure.

Base verb	Past tense	Past participle	Base verb	Past tense	Past participle
a begin		begun	**h** go	went	
b bite	bit		**i** grow		grown
c blow		blown	**j** hang	hung	
d dream	dreamed/ dreamt		**k** know	knew	
e drink		drunk	**l** see	saw	
f drive	drove		**m** wear		worn
g forgive		forgiven			

3 Underline the correct **irregular past participle** in the following sentences.

a That was how the mistake had arisen/arised.

b With one accord, though nothing of the kind had been planned beforehand, they flinged/ flung themselves upon their tormentors.

c He had became/become much disheartened after losing money in a lawsuit, and had taken to drinking more than was good for him.

d Stone would have to be carried and built/builded up into walls

- **e** His tail had grown/grew rigid and twitched sharply from side to side, a sign in him of intense mental activity.
- **f** She had began/begun to move when Farmer Jones came in.

4 Complete these sentences using the correct **past participle**. Mark each either *R* for regular or *I* for irregular.

For example: Orwell wrote that *Animal Farm* was the first book in which he had (try) __tried__ to fuse political purpose and artistic purpose into one whole. __R__

- **a** Tsar Nicholas II, the monarch of Russia, was forced to abdicate the throne that his family had (hold) ______________ for three centuries. ______
- **b** The publisher, Jonathan Cape, had (accept) ______________ *Animal Farm*, only to then reject the book. ______
- **c** The publisher had (provide) ______________ space for a preface in the author's proofs. ______
- **d** This unification of economic systems allowed Russia to experience the affluence it had (know) ______________ before World War I. ______
- **e** Immediately prior to his writing, Orwell had (quit) ______________ the BBC. ______

Subject–verb agreement

A **sentence** is a group of words containing a **verb** and usually a **subject** and **predicate**. There is a unit coming up about sentences (Unit 6), but here we will look at the basic structure of a simple sentence with a focus on **verbs** within it.

- The **subject** of a sentence is **who** or **what** the sentence is about (usually a noun). The **predicate** is the rest of the sentence which tells us about the subject. The predicate includes the **verb**; for example, **Mr Jones** (subject)/**is** *the farm owner* (predicate). Asking **who** or **what** will help you **identify** the sentence's **subject**.
- A **subject** may also include **adjectives** or **other words around the noun** to form a noun group (as you saw in Unit 1); for example, *the prize Middle White* **boar**.
- **Subjects** are usually the **first word** in a sentence, but they are not always; for example, *In addition, Orwell criticises the ways that leaders use violence to frighten people.* Here *Orwell* is the subject.
- Most **subjects** and **verbs** are very **close** to each other in a sentence; for example, *George Orwell wrote* Animal Farm. However, sometimes subjects are **distant** from their corresponding verbs within sentences; for example, **Mr Jones, of the Manor Farm, had locked the hen-houses for the night, but was too drunk to remember to shut the pop-holes**. The verbs *had locked* and *was* relate back to the sentence subject *Mr Jones.*
- **Separating** a subject and verb with too much extra information may cause **confusion** for readers who have to re-read the sentences to understand the ideas; for example, *Mr Jones,* **who in the aftermath of a very damaging lawsuit became an alcoholic and harsh ruler over the animals,** *lurched across the yard, kicked off his boots at the back door, and drew himself a last glass of beer.*
- **Verbs** must **agree in number** with their singular or plural subject; for example, *Mr Jones* **drinks** *to excess and* **loses** *the farm* (not 'Mr Jones drink to excess and lose the farm').

5 Underline the **subjects** of the underlined verbs in each sentence. It may be more than one word, and it may not be the first word.

- **a** Clover, a stout motherly mare approaching middle life, had never quite got her figure back after her fourth foal.
- **b** From the very beginning, it was clear that Mollie was not going to last long in the rebellion.
- **c** In different situations, people and societies can become desensitised to deception and violence.
- **d** The poor burdened workers, oppressed by capitalism, wanted their dignity restored.
- **e** Almost instantly after *Animal Farm* was published, it became the subject of controversy.

6 In the following examples, circle the **verbs** that correspond to the underlined subject.

For example: I (am) 12 years old and (have had) over 400 children.

- **a** Those ribbons are the badge of slavery.
- **b** Everyone fled to his own sleeping-place and settled down in the straw.
- **c** No animal will live in a house, or sleep in a bed, or wear clothes, or drink alcohol, or smoke tobacco, or touch money, or engage in trade.
- **d** All the other male pigs on the farm were porkers, who had very round cheeks, twinkling eyes, nimble movements, and shrill voices.

7 Underline the **correct verb** in each sentence to ensure **subject–verb agreement**.

For example: Moses (is/are) Mr Jones's special pet, a spy and a tale-bearer and also a clever talker.

- **a** Everybody (want/wants) a happy ending for the animals.
- **b** Despite living in fear, many (is/are) prepared to make a stand.
- **c** Nobody (needs/need) the food or supplies but they (takes/take) it anyway.
- **d** Everyone (love/loves) the book, despite being made to read it, and (is/are) looking forward to seeing the film version.
- **e** The animals, supposedly ending the days of extreme hunger and labour, (rebels/rebel) by driving out Mr Jones, and (remove/removes) him from power.

Punctuation in use

***Animal Farm*, a modern fable by George Orwell, is about a group of animals who banish the humans from the farm on which they live.** It is Old Major who stirs the other animals on Mr Jones's Manor Farm to accept Animalism. They are driven to create a society that is fair and governed by individuals with integrity. **Orwell felt that a farm where all 'Animals Are Equal' would solve many social and economic problems, but he also knew that such a system would be difficult to maintain**, since some animals would act on the principle that 'Some Are More Equal Than Others'.

About punctuation

Commas are often used to **make meaning clear**, particularly in long sentences, by:

- **separating long chunks of extra information** from the rest of the sentence; for example, ***Animal Farm*, a modern fable by George Orwell, is about a group of animals who banish the humans from the farm on which they live.**
- **separating two or more long statements** joined by words such as *and, but* and *or*; for example, **Orwell felt that a farm where all 'Animals Are Equal' would solve many social and economic problems, but he also knew that such a system would be difficult to maintain.**
- **helping to avoid confusion and misunderstanding.** Look at these sentences: *I enjoy cooking my family and my pets* and *I enjoy cooking, my family and my pets.* The omission of a comma in the first example creates a disturbing idea that is very different from the meaning in the second example.

1 Put **commas** in these sentences to mark off the long chunks of extra information. Remember to place commas both before and after the extra words.

- **a** The revolution in *Animal Farm* like other revolutions in history was initiated by a powerful desire for change.
- **b** Aspects of *Animal Farm* that are historically linked to Soviet history such as the revolution and the failings of the government are presented symbolically throughout the novel.
- **c** With one accord though nothing of the kind had been planned beforehand they flung themselves upon their tormentors.
- **d** Word had spread among the animals during the day that Old Major an old and respected prize boar had a strange dream and wanted to speak to them.
- **e** The owners of the farms next door to Animal Farm including Mr Pilkington of Foxwood and Mr Frederick of Pinchfield are concerned that the revolution might spread to their own farms.

2 Put the missing **commas** where needed in these long statements.

- **a** The animals believe life on the farm has improved to some extent but they have less food than ever.
- **b** Clover made a sort of wall round them with her great foreleg and the ducklings nestled down inside it then promptly fell asleep.
- **c** Snowball tells Mollie she shouldn't want sugar and ribbons so she tries hard to give them up.
- **d** At the meeting everyone is allowed to voice their opinions and vote but only the pigs seem to be allowed to make any changes.
- **e** The other animals grumble but Squealer explains that the pigs are crucial to the running of the farm and they need the milk and apples to stay healthy.

3 Tick (✔) the sentence with the clearest **meaning**.

a Before leaving the animals demolished the food.
Before leaving, the animals demolished the food.

b To Frederick, Pilkington appeared confident in reaching a compromise.
To Frederick Pilkington appeared confident in reaching a compromise.

c Everybody they thought would win won.
Everybody they thought would win, won.

d Animals who can, take advantage of those inferior to them.
Animals who can take advantage of those inferior to them.

4 Remembering all **comma** rules, tick (✔) sentences that use commas correctly. Rewrite the others correctly.

a The pigs, despite being the greediest instruct the other animals.

b The animals destroy all whips, nose rings, reins, and all other instruments that have been used to suppress them.

c The animals also agree that no animal shall ever enter the farmhouse, and that no animal shall have contact with humans.

d Napoleon, who had not fought at all, takes a medal.

e Now comrades what is the nature of this life of ours?

f The other animals remember that there is a commandment that forbids sleeping in beds, and so they go to the big barn to look at the commandments.

5 Remembering all the rules about **commas** so far, punctuate this text correctly.

> The animals of Manor Farm had always been oppressed under the management of Mr Jones. They grow to accept their situation as part of the natural order of life but it is Old Major a prize-winning boar who shares his desire for change with the other animals. It is three young pigs called Snowball Napoleon and Squealer who transform Old Major's dream into a political ideology called Animalism. Initially the pigs supervise the farming work and all the animals work hard but there are worrying signs that the pigs distinguish themselves as different from the other animals. The promises of free time heat or machinery to help never eventuate.

UNIT FIVE

Mother India

Focus

Adjectives and adverbs; capital letters

Grammar in use

Adapted from *Mother India* by Katherine Mayo (1937)

Calcutta, **second-largest** city in the **British** Empire, spreads right **along** the Ganges, at the top of the Bay of Bengal. Calcutta is **big**, **western** and **modern**, with public buildings, monuments, parks, gardens, hospitals, museums, university, courts of law, hotels, offices, shops, all of which might belong to a prosperous American city; and all backed by an Indian town of temples, mosques, bazaars and intricate courtyards and alleys that has somehow created itself despite the **rectangular** lines shown on the map.

In the courts and alleys and bazaars there are **many** bookstalls, where **narrow-chested, near-sighted** young Bengali students, in native dress, brood over piles of **fly-blown** Russian pamphlets. You cannot see the street from Government House Gardens, for the walls are **high**. But if you could, you would see it filled with traffic—motor traffic, mostly—limousines, touring cars, taxis and private machines.

About grammar

Adjectives describe or give information about **nouns** and **pronouns** by **identifying** or **describing** them in more detail. There are various types of adjectives.

- **Qualitative adjectives** identify **qualities** of people or things; for example, *Calcutta is* **big**, **western** *and* **modern**; *despite the* **rectangular** *lines; the walls are* **high**.
- **Quantitative adjectives**, such as *two, twenty, many, some, all, most, few* and *several,* add information about **how much** or **how many**; for example, *there are* **many** *bookstalls.*
- **Classifying adjectives** are used to divide people or things into particular groups, types or classes; for example, *Calcutta,* **second-largest** *city in the* **British** *Empire.*
- **Emphasising adjectives** are used to emphasise your feelings about the person or thing you are talking about; for example, *The trip was a* **complete** *success; The guide was an* **utter** *delight.*
- **Possessive adjectives**, such as *my, your, his, her, its, our* and *their*, show ownership; for example, *I can't wait to tell you about* **our** *trip*. You read about these in Unit 2.
- **Demonstrative adjectives** include *that, this, those* and *these*; for example, **This** *book was written in 1937* and **These** *kinds of books provide a vivid image of places we have never seen.*

We sometimes make adjectives by joining two words together with a **hyphen.** They may be qualitative or classifying adjectives; for example, **narrow-chested, fly-blown, near-sighted.**

We also make adjectives **by adding** *ing* to a verb; for example, *There is a* **startling** *increase in the number of visitors to India* and *There were many* **challenging** *aspects to my trip.*

Comparative and superlative adjectives allow you to compare two or more things. A **comparative adjective** compares two things; for example, *India is* **larger** *than France*, and *I think India is* **more interesting** *than anywhere else*. A **superlative** adjective compares more than two; for example, *India has one of the* **largest** *populations* and *We saw the* **most interesting** *things*.

Adverbs are short phrases or words which **add meaning to** (or **modify**) verbs, adjectives and other adverbs.

- **Adverbs of time,** such as *now, yesterday* and *weekly,* and **frequency,** such as *always, often, never, rarely* and *now,* describe **when or how often something happens**; for example, *Just as you see those doing* **now** and *We* **often** *rested in the heat of the afternoon.*
- **Adverbs of place** such as *here, there, around* and *everywhere* provide information about the **location** where the action of the verb is being carried out; for example, *spreads right* **along** and *come* **here**.
- **Adverbs of manner** such as *well, quickly, softly* and *loudly* give more information about **the way** in which an event or action takes place; for example, *The boat travelled* **slowly** *down the Ganges.*
- **Adverbs of degree** such as *almost, extremely, really, terribly* and *much* give more information about the **extent** of an action or the **degree** to which an action is performed; for example, *The city was* **absolutely** *wonderful* and *We felt* **incredibly** *lucky to visit there.* While most adverbs modify verbs, adverbs of degree can also **add meaning to adjectives**; for example, *a* **very** *prosperous city, a* **rather** *anaemic person, a* **really** *bad journey.*

Unlike adjectives, the **comparative of an adverb** is usually formed with *more* and the **superlative** with *most*, and not by adding *er* and *est*; for example, *The traffic moved* **more slowly** *with each hour* and *I visited the* **most beautifully** *decorated buildings in the country.*

In most cases, an adverb is formed by adding *ly* to an adjective; however, you often need to change the spelling. If the adjective ends in *y*, replace the *y* with *i* and add *ly*; for example, *easy* → *easily*. If the adjective ends in *able, ible* or *le*, replace the *e* with a *y*; for example, *probable* → *probably, terrible* → *terribly, gentle* → *gently.*

Boost your grammar skills

1 Underline the **adjectives** and circle the **adverbs** in each sentence.

- **a** India contains many official languages, and locals over there speak regional dialects.
- **b** You should visit a silk factory while you are there.
- **c** The religious temple in Mysore rightly insists that you remove footwear before entering.
- **d** Sacred cows and other different animals frequently roam some temple grounds.
- **e** Bumpy rickshaw rides and long-haul flights from Australia can really affect your nerves.

2 Underline the **adjectives** in the following sentences and identify the type of adjective. The corresponding nouns are bolded.

For example: India is a large **country** by area. qualitative

a Our visit to India will be an absolute **adventure**. ______

b A variety of religions help shape the region's diverse **culture**. ______

c The Indian **subcontinent** is identified by its commercial and cultural **wealth**.

______

d An open-minded approach is needed when travelling to new and different **places**.

______

e We had a brilliant and awesome **experience** in India! ______

f These **suitcases** will be heavy by the end of our journey. ______

g Several **acquaintances** have travelled to India and their **trip** was also enjoyable.

______ and ______

3 Place each of the following **adverbs** in the column for its type.

yesterday fast much once below honestly almost completely often here cheerfully well quite a few months ago over there everywhere

Manner	Degree	Place	Time
quietly	very	outside	usually

4 Underline each **adverb**. Circle the **verb** or **adjective** it modifies (adds meaning to).

For example: India usually (exports) software to 90 countries.

a Algebra, trigonometry and calculus originally came from India.

b There are about 1.6 million people happily employed by Indian Railway.

c In the last 1000 years, India has never invaded another country.

d Yoga has its origins in India and has existed constantly for 5000 years.

e India is considered a very exciting travel destination.

5 Write two **adverbs** that could be used to describe each **verb** or **adjective**. Try to use a variety of different types of adverbs.

a sit ______ ______

b laugh ______ ______

c move ______ ______

d work ______ ______

e eat ______ ______

f stand ______ ______

g amusing ______ ______

h world-famous ______ ______

6 Turn the following **adjectives** into **adverbs**.

a mysterious ______________________ b terrible ______________________

c full ______________________ d inexpensive ______________________

e angry ______________________ f thankful ______________________

g true ______________________ h easy ______________________

7 Complete the following sentences with the correct **comparative or superlative adverb or adjective**.

For example: When travelling, I usually get up earlier (early) than my brother.

a This journey is ______________________ (interesting) than the one I took last year.

b That was ______________________ (good) train trip I have ever experienced.

c Calcutta was even ______________________ (fascinating) than Bangladesh.

d I finished planning my itinerary ______________________ (fast) than my companions.

e That hotel was ______________________ (expensive) in the entire region.

Confusing adjectives and adverbs

It is important that you know whether you need an **adjective** or an **adverb** in the sentences you use. Remember: adjectives add information about nouns and pronouns, and adverbs add information about verbs, adjectives and other adverbs. In the following sentence pairs, the first sentences contain **adjectives**, and the second sentences contain **adverbs**.

He's a **wonderful** *writer. He writes* **wonderfully**.

He's a **quick** *learner. He can learn* **quickly**.

She's a **careful** *writer. She writes* **carefully**.

She's a **good** *worker. She works* **well.**

There are a few words that have the same adjectival and adverbial form, such as *fast, straight* and *inside*; for example, *The* **fast** *train arrives at noon. The train went so* **fast** *it made me sick.*

8 Circle the correct word in the following sentences. Write next to each if you have chosen an **adjective or adverb**.

a He has done (well/good) in planning the trip's details. ______________________

b I felt (good/well) about the decisions I had made during the journey. ______________________

c The trip ended (bad/badly) when we lost our luggage. ______________________

d I felt (badly/bad) about some of the poverty we observed. ______________________

e I held the train's handrail (tight/tightly) as it sped round each curve. ______________________

f My jumper was a (tight/tightly) fit as I held my travel documents under it. ______________________

g We drove (quickly/quick) in order to make the plane. ______________________

h It was only a (quick/quickly) flight so I knew we wouldn't be too tired. ______________________

i I find travelling (real/really) exciting. ______________________

j I hope to find some (real/really) Indian cultural outfits. ______________________

Punctuation in use

Kolkata, known historically in **English** as **Calcutta**, is the capital of the Indian state of West Bengal. Located on the east bank of the Hooghly River, it is the principal commercial, cultural and educational centre of **East India**, while the **Port of Kolkata** is India's oldest operating port. Kolkata's recorded history began in 1690 with the arrival of the **English East India Company**. **Job Charnock**, an administrator who worked for the Company, is traditionally credited as the founder of the city.

Adapted from http://en.wikipedia.org/wiki/Kolkata

About punctuation

- We use **capital letters** to begin every sentence and **full stops** to end all sentences that are statements (that is, they do not ask a question).
- All **proper nouns** begin with capital letters; for example, **Kolkata**, **English**, **Calcutta**.
- Capital letters start names, titles, months, days of the week, organisations, institutions, brand names, religions, languages, nationalities and important festivals; for example, **Job Charnock**, **English East India Company**.
- All **main words** in a proper noun need to begin with capital letters; for example, **East India**. However, we don't use capitals for little words like *and, of, in* and *the* unless they appear as the first word of the title; for example, **Port of Kolkata**; *I saw a great film set in India called* **The Darjeeling Limited**.
- Some nouns may be **proper nouns** in some sentences and **common nouns** in others; for example, *We are waiting for* **Deputy Mayor** *Alum. She is the* **deputy mayor** *of Calcutta.*
- The seasons *summer, autumn, winter* and *spring* are considered common nouns unless they appear in a title; for example, *The* **Winter** *Olympics.*

Boost your punctuation skills

1 Rewrite the following sentences with the correct **capital letters**.

a A popular indian film is *the legend of bhagat singh.*

____

b The high court is located on strand road.

____

c The financial hub is home to the calcutta stock exchange.

____

d Among calcutta's smaller communities are chinese, tamils, armenians and greeks.

____

e mother teresa of calcutta was awarded the nobel peace prize in 1979.

____

f the black hole of calcutta was a small dungeon in the old fort william.

____

2 Underline any word that is missing a **capital letter** in the following sentences.

- **a** Bankim chandra chattopadhyay was one of the earliest bengali novelists.
- **b** The Calcutta book Fair is an annual fair showcasing local books.
- **c** the Indian museum houses large collections that showcase indian natural history and Indian art.
- **d** The government college of art and Craft was founded in 1864.
- **e** the academy of fine Arts and other art galleries hold regular art exhibitions.

3 Write on the lines any words with missing **capital letters**.

- **a** *Sharodotsab* is also known as the 'Festival of autumn'.

  ____

- **b** Gurbux singh was a medallist in the 1964 summer olympics.

  ____

- **c** a former policeman, mayor chattergee was born in kolkata.

  ____

- **d** Major festivals usually take place during the autumn period from september to october.

  ____

- **e** Rains are brought by the bay of Bengal branch of the south-west summer monsoon.

  ____

4 Tick (✔) the sentences that use **capital letters** correctly.

- **a** Kolkata is the main commercial and financial hub of East and North-East India.
- **b** The Ordnance factories Board of the ministry of Defence is also headquartered in the city.
- **c** The Kolkata Police, headed by a police commissioner, is overseen by the West Bengal Ministry of Home Affairs.
- **d** Kolkata has rail and road connectivity with Dhaka, Capital of Bangladesh.

5 Edit the following text by adding **capital letters** where they are needed.

> Many people have asked me what draws me to kolkata, and it's a difficult question to answer. I received a book with daily quotes from the blessed teresa of Calcutta called 'the joy in Loving'. I remember reading one entry which described a young girl visiting Kolkata from paris. As soon as I finished school, I decided I would go to Kolkata to volunteer. it was many miles away from my all-girls school in rural england. I began working in a dispensary and led a group of volunteers painting the park at shishu Bhavan. Since that first visit, I have volunteered elsewhere with the missionaries of Charity.
>
> Adapted from 'Volunteering with the Missionaries of Charity in Kolkata' by Verity Worthington, Volunteer, http://www.motherteresa.org/07_family/volunteering/v_cal.html

Revision Test 1

Grammar

Shade one circle to show the correct answer for questions 1–8.

1 Which of the underlined words in this sentence is a noun?

Green gardening relies on fresh manure, compost and biological pest control.

- ◯ Green
- ◯ fresh
- ◯ compost
- ◯ biological

2 Which word is a concrete noun?

- ◯ very
- ◯ glad
- ◯ puppy
- ◯ ambition

3 Which word is **not** an abstract noun?

- ◯ intelligence
- ◯ pyramid
- ◯ power
- ◯ faith

4 Underline the noun group in the following sentence.

His pants were made of the finest green patterned silk.

5 Which pronoun correctly completes the sentence?

Those shoes I gave ________________ last year have lasted her a long time.

- ◯ me
- ◯ she
- ◯ her
- ◯ them

6 Which word is **not** a demonstrative pronoun?

- ◯ this
- ◯ these
- ◯ his
- ◯ those

7 Which word does the pronoun *it* refer to?

I put the cat outside, but the rain started falling heavily, so I let it in again.

- ◯ cat
- ◯ outside
- ◯ rain
- ◯ I

8 Which sentence is correct?

- ◯ None is visiting the museum this year.
- ◯ If everyone take a small section home, we will be finished quickly.
- ◯ Both are going to make it, but they're going to be late.

9 Use the correct reflexive pronoun in the following sentence.

The students enjoyed ________________ immensely at the museum

10 Circle the two underlined verbs that are helping verbs in this sentence.

When I see her again she will have contacted her sister.

Shade one circle to show the correct answer for questions 11–27.

11 Which group of verbs shows continuous action?

- ◯ will be looking
- ◯ have been located
- ◯ might be stolen
- ◯ should eat

12 Which line contains a verb group?

- ◯ I love my little sister
- ◯ We would have booked
- ◯ a red, shiny, bright car
- ◯ She is so very funny

13 Which sentence is written in the active voice?

- ◯ The book has been read by millions of people all over the world.
- ◯ Millions of people all over the world have read the book.

14 Which underlined word is a finite (complete) verb?

After running to the station, the student bought a ticket to travel on the bus.

(Underlined options: running ◯ · bought ◯ · to travel ◯)

15 Which underlined word is a non-finite (incomplete) verb?

The teacher said: 'Take every opportunity to learn.'

(Underlined options: said ◯ · to learn ◯)

16 Which underlined *ing* word is a noun?

While studying helps you become a better student, it's not healthy to always be studying.

(Underlined options: studying ◯ · studying ◯)

17 Which sentence does **not** have a finite verb?

- ◯ She likes to sing every day and will sing at the end-of-year concert.
- ◯ Singing three songs and playing the piano at the end-of-year concert.
- ◯ Since she is singing at the end-of-year concert, we will be buying some tickets.

18 Which sentence is correct?

- ◯ Winning was my most happiest moment.
- ◯ The coffee here is better than the coffee from Paul Street.
- ◯ I think this restaurant was more better than the other.

19 Which sentence is correct?

- ◯ Mum freaked out when we bought the spiders into the house.
- ◯ I had forgot to bring the parcel so will need to post it instead.
- ◯ The boy had drunk too much lemonade and was feeling ill as a result.

20 Which sentence shows subject–verb agreement?

- ◯ The cheese and tomato is delicious on my sandwich.
- ◯ Few knows what it really takes to succeed in the industry.
- ◯ Each of them gets a trophy for winning the premiership.

21 Which underlined word in this sentence is **not** an adjective?

This beautiful sandy beach has two pools for small children to swim safely in.

◯ ◯ ◯ ◯ ◯

22 Which underlined word in this sentence is **not** an adjective?

An exciting new museum has opened and five friends have already visited it.

◯ ◯ ◯ ◯ ◯

23 Which underlined word in this sentence is an adverb of time?

We often visit relatives during holidays, but Mum really likes to leave quickly.

◯ ◯ ◯ ◯ ◯

24 Which underlined word in this sentence is an adverb of place?

The leaves always seem to fall everywhere but they are actually rather nice.

◯ ◯ ◯

25 Which sentence uses the correct tense?

- ◯ As I started the computer, my log-in screen greets me.
- ◯ She is studying at this school for the last three years.
- ◯ As soon as we receive your payment, we will ship the parcel to you.

26 Which sentence shows correct use of comparative adjectives?

- ◯ My book was better than yours.
- ◯ My book was more good than yours.
- ◯ My book was more better than yours.

27 Which sentence is correct?

- ◯ I asked the driver to get there quick.
- ◯ I asked the driver to get there quickly.
- ◯ I asked the driver to get there more quick.

Punctuation

In questions 1–5, insert the missing commas.

1 The house looked huge dark isolated and scary in the moonlight.

2 There were no people animals cars or houses anywhere to be seen.

3 Some people think you should finish school go to university travel and then think about getting a job.

4 The package small and compact fit neatly into his back pocket.

5 I know in fact she left the country early this morning.

In questions 6–12, which sentence is correctly punctuated? Shade one circle.

6
- ◯ Listen to me Henry when I'm talking to you!
- ◯ Listen to me Henry, when I'm talking to you!
- ◯ Listen to me, Henry, when I'm talking to you!

7
- ◯ Would you mind passing me the sugar, please?
- ◯ Would you mind passing me the sugar please?
- ◯ Would you mind, passing me the sugar please?

8
- ◯ You will be there for my party won't you?
- ◯ You will be there for my party, won't you?
- ◯ You, will be there for my party won't you?

9
- ◯ The test won't be as easy the next time, I suppose.
- ◯ The test won't be as easy, the next time I suppose.
- ◯ The test won't be as easy the next time I suppose.

In questions 10–11, insert the missing commas.

10 The poem written during the late 19th century remains popular today.

11 The student knew she had completed all the work necessary and that the assignment was placed neatly in her bag.

In questions 12–15, which sentence is correctly punctuated? Shade one circle.

12
- ◯ Ballarat is a city located on the Yarrowee River and the lower western plains of the Great Dividing Range in the state of Victoria, Australia.
- ◯ Ballarat is a city located on the Yarrowee river and the lower western plains of the great Dividing Range in the state of Victoria, Australia.
- ◯ Ballarat is a city located on the Yarrowee River and the lower western plains of the great dividing range in the state of Victoria, Australia.

13
- ◯ Helen Clark, as Prime minister of New Zealand, served three terms from 1999 to 2008.
- ◯ Helen Clark, as Prime Minister of New Zealand, served three terms from 1999 to 2008.
- ◯ Helen Clark, as prime minister of New zealand, served three terms from 1999 to 2008.

14
- ◯ The winter Olympics were held in Calgary in 2010.
- ◯ The Winter olympics were held in Calgary in 2010.
- ◯ The Winter Olympics were held in Calgary in 2010.

15
- ◯ Malala Yousafzai, from Pakistan, was announced as the co-recipient of the 2014 Nobel Peace Prize.
- ◯ Malala Yousafzai, from pakistan, was announced as the co-recipient of the 2014 Nobel Peace Prize.
- ◯ Malala Yousafzai, from Pakistan, was announced as the co-recipient of the 2014 Nobel peace prize.

UNIT SIX

Renewable energy sources

Simple and compound sentences; brackets and dashes

Grammar in use

Energy exists freely in nature. Some energy exists infinitely and never runs out. This is called **renewable energy. The rest have finite (limited) amounts and they will run out one day.** This is **non-renewable energy. Renewable energy includes biomass, wind, hydropower, geothermal and solar power.** Renewable energy can be converted into electricity, which is stored and transported to our homes for use. **Offshore resource wind speed is greater than on land, so it can contribute more energy. Interesting developments in renewables are happening and these may lead to good, cheap sources of power in the future.**

About grammar

Simple and compound sentences

- A **sentence** is a group of words that can make complete sense on its own. It contains a **verb** and usually a **subject** and **predicate**.
- A **simple sentence** consists of one clause, which is one unit of meaning, generally with one verb; for example, *Energy* **exists** *freely in nature.* Sometimes a simple sentence may have two verbs; for example, *We can* **store** *and* **transport** *energy.*
- The **basic elements** of a sentence are the **subject** and the **verb**. The **subject** is a noun, pronoun or a noun group that names a person, place or thing; for example, **Energy** *exists freely in nature*; **Renewable energy** *includes biomass, wind, hydropower, geothermal and solar power.*
- The **predicate** is the rest of the sentence which tells us about the subject. The predicate includes the **verb**; for example, **Energy** (subject) **exists** *freely in nature* (predicate). Asking **who** or **what** will help you **identify** the sentence's **subject**. You read about this on page 19.
- The predicate often, but not always, includes an **object**—the person or thing that the verb acts upon; for example, *Renewable energy* (subject) *includes* **biomass, wind, hydropower, geothermal and solar power** (object). *Energy* (subject) *exists freely in nature* (no object as the verb *exists* does not act upon anything).
- When two or more **simple sentences** are joined together to make a longer sentence, they become a **compound sentence**. A compound sentence contains **two or more** clauses of equal importance. Each clause contains **one verb** and is **independent**—that is, each clause can stand alone and make sense; for example, *The rest* **have** *finite (limited) amounts and they* **will run** *out one day.*
- **Compound sentences can be made from more than two independent clauses** and we often combine three or four; for example, *The rest* **have** *finite (limited) amounts and they* **will run** *out one day but technology* **is helping** *the situation.*
- The **separate clauses** in **compound sentences** are joined together with **coordinating conjunctions** such as *and, but, yet, or, nor* and (sometimes) *so*. They link clauses and sentences of equal rank.

* The **noun** that appears in the **first clause** of a compound sentence may be **replaced** by a **pronoun** in the **second**; for example, **Interesting developments** *in renewables are happening and* **these** [interesting developments] *may lead to good, cheap sources of power in the future.*
* The **noun** or **pronoun** in the **second clause** is often **omitted** if it is the same as the one in the first clause. If the conjunction is *and, or* or *then*, you **do not usually repeat the subject**; for example, **Some energy exists infinitely and** [it] **never runs out**. If the conjunction is *but, so* or *yet*, it is usual to **repeat the subject** or use a **pronoun**; for example, **Offshore resource** *wind speed is greater than on land, so* **it** *can contribute more energy.*

Boost your grammar skills

1 Write *S* for **simple sentence** or *C* for **compound sentence** next to each sentence below.

- **a** Heating water uses energy. ______
- **b** Buy toys at yard sales and you can save energy and money. ______
- **c** Aluminium can be recycled many times over. ______
- **d** It only takes a minute to recycle and it saves energy. ______
- **e** The average home spends 11 per cent of its electricity bill on lighting. ______
- **f** The industrial sector uses 30 per cent of total Australian energy consumption. ______

2 Tick (✔) each group of words that is a **sentence**. Cross (✘) the groups that are not.

- **a** You should pay attention to the energy guide label.
- **b** Can be made using a very simple generator.
- **c** Quantities of water through a big wheel.
- **d** Renewable energy is derived from natural processes.
- **e** Energy-saving roof solar panels.
- **f** The most powerful source of light.
- **g** Green is good.

3 Underline the **independent clauses** in the following sentences. There may be more than one.

- **a** Operate the appliance each week and then test it.
- **b** Buy an efficient refrigerator or you will regret it.
- **c** Lights and television use electrical energy so you should turn them off.
- **d** Recycling has many benefits and reduces the amount of paper in landfills yet there are still many trees lost.
- **e** Renewable sources are either carbon neutral or they do not produce greenhouse gases and so they are much less harmful to the environment.

4 Join these two independent clauses to make **compound sentences** using **coordinating conjunctions**.

- **a** Automobiles damage the environment ________________ people love to drive them.
- **b** You could purchase fewer goods ________________ buy only what you need.
- **c** Most people worry about air pollution from auto exhaust ________________ they also worry about traffic congestion.

d Take time to recycle ________________ there will be consequences.

e Reusable items can be expensive ________________ you will save natural resources.

5 Change the **coordinating conjunction** in each sentence so that it makes better sense.

a Energy sources must be reconsidered but the environment will continue to suffer. ________

b Reducing, reusing and recycling help protect the environment yet save money, energy and natural resources. ________

c Energy can be made from non-renewable energy sources or there is a cost to the environment. ________

d You can't make more non-renewable sources but can you invent them. ________

e Burning fossil fuels produces greenhouse gases so many businesses have no choice about using them. ________

6 Insert the corresponding **noun** or **pronoun** in the second clause to show the relationship between clauses. Some clauses may require no noun or pronoun at all.

a You use a lot of electricity every day and ________________ should use only what you need.

b Oil is the third leading fuel and so ________________ is used often for home heating.

c A solar energy system adds value to your home or business and ________________ will be much more attractive to buyers as power costs increase.

d Trains are lighter and stronger but ________________ aren't cost effective.

e Choosing a solar panel on price alone is not wise and ________________ may end up not choosing the best one for your home environment.

7 For each of the following sentences, identify the word(s) in **bold** as a verb, subject or object.

a **Energy** is used in every step of paper making. ________________

b We need energy to cook our **lunch and dinner**. ________________

c **Nuclear power stations** use a radioactive fuel called uranium. ________________

d Engineers **drill** down to the reservoirs. ________________

e The blades of the wind turbine **catch** the wind. ________________

f Renewable energy can be called **green energy**. ________________

g **Windmills and generators** have a lot in common. ________________

8 Make the following text flow more easily by combining some short sentences into **compound sentences**. Remove repetitive nouns or pronouns. There is more than one way to do this. Don't forget that **compound sentences can be made up of more than two independent clauses**. Use your own paper.

> Renewable energy is healthy and environmentally friendly. Renewable energy can be used without depleting the environment. All forms of energy are expensive. As time and technologies progress, renewable energy generally gets cheaper. Fossil fuels generally get more expensive. There are ways to save energy. Open the curtains and use the sunlight instead of turning on the lights. Turn off the dishwasher right before the drying cycle. Let the dishes air dry. There are a lot more ways to save energy. It's important that everyone pitches in to conserve energy.

Punctuation in use

Energy can be called renewable when its source cannot run out (**like the sun**) or it can be replaced (like wood, as trees can be replanted). It can also be called renewable when the **energy sources are carbon neutral**. This means they **do not produce** greenhouse gases. **Renewable energy must also not pollute the environment—air, land or water**.

Edmond Becquerel (1820–1891) is known for discovering **the photovoltaic effect (how electricity can be generated from sunlight).** ***Science and Optics*** **observes that, 'He [Edmond] was particularly intrigued by light—it formed his life's work!—and he embarked on in-depth studies of the subject.'** Today, the **International Energy Agency (IEA)** has said that solar power generators will have the capacity within 50 years to produce most of the world's electricity.

About punctuation

We use dashes — and brackets **( )** to add extra information to a sentence. Brackets are also called **parentheses** and they are always used in pairs; for example, **(like the sun)**.

- Brackets are **more formal** than dashes. You are more likely to use **dashes** in an email or a narrative text. **Brackets** are more likely to be used in academic texts like essays and reports.
- Dashes can be generally used to **set apart extra information**; for example, *Renewable energy must also not pollute the environment*—**air, land or water**.
- Dashes can also be used to **enclose expressions of feelings** or **opinions** about a topic; for example, *'He was particularly intrigued by light*—**it formed his life's work!**—*and he embarked on in-depth studies of the subject.'*
- Brackets are often used to provide **explanations** or to add **abbreviated forms**; for example, *the photovoltaic effect* **(how electricity can be generated from sunlight)**; *International Energy Agency* **(IEA)**.
- Square brackets are used to enclose words that you add to a **direct quotation**; for example, *Science and Optics reports that, 'He* **[Edmond]** *was particularly intrigued by light.'*
- Brackets are also used to enclose **dates**; for example, *Edmond Becquerel* **(1820–1891)**. The date is something you want to tell the reader, but it isn't a necessary part of the sentence.
- We sometimes use brackets to enclose larger chunks of text, such as complete sentences or paragraphs. If the brackets surround a **complete sentence**, the bracketed sentence needs to be punctuated as a whole sentence usually would, with a capital letter and a full stop; for example, *energy sources are carbon neutral.* (*This means they do not produce greenhouse gases.*) The full stop appears **inside** the brackets if the bracket contains a complete sentence. If not, it should be placed outside the bracket.

Do not overuse brackets and dashes in your writing; commas will often work just as well in maintaining the flow of your ideas.

1 Place **brackets** where needed in the following sentences.

a Clean energy doesn't emit carbon dioxide CO_2.

b Solar energy is renewable this means that energy from the sun never ends

c Charles F Brush 1849–1929 invented the world's first automatically operated wind turbine.

d Renewable energy uses natural resources that can be renewed replaced without harming the environment.

e Polyethylene terephthalate PET has a wide range of uses including synthetic fibres and containers for food, beverage and other liquids.

2 Use **dashes** in the following sentences to **set apart extra information** or to **enclose feelings or opinions**. Write them above where you think they should go.

a The topic of alternative energy encompasses a range of sub-topics wind, water, nuclear and geothermal energy.

b Many items in my home require electricity to run TV set, microwave oven, electric kettle, computer and refrigerator.

c When the sun shines and we hope it does! it can heat the water and cool the house.

d The average person is said to throw away I can't believe it almost two kilograms of rubbish every day.

e There are a number of ways to become more environmentally friendly recycle, conserve water and fuel and make other choices that lessen your impact on the environment.

3 Place **brackets** around the **explanations** in the following sentences.

a Another form of geothermal energy is called hot rock this is where water is pumped below the surface to areas of hot rock.

b A landfill site also known as a tip, dump, rubbish dump or dumping ground is a site for the disposal of waste materials by burial.

c The term windmill comes from 'to mill' meaning 'to grind'.

d Charles F Brush inventor of the wind turbine was raised on a farm about seven kilometres from Cleveland, Ohio.

e The gas generated by landfill as it rots is another form of renewable or 'green' energy.

4 Tick (✔) the correctly punctuated **sentences** and rewrite the others correctly on your own paper.

a Solar photovoltaic PV technology generates electricity from sunlight.

b As the community becomes more environmentally aware (by changing their lifestyles) landfill will be reduced.

c Windmills are used in many countries US, India, Germany and France.

d The turbine's diameter was 17 metres (50 feet), it had 144 rotor blades made of cedar wood, and it generated about 12 kilowatts (kW) of power.

5 Edit the following text by inserting **dashes** and **brackets** where they are missing.

> Many people are saving money on their power bills by changing from incandescent light bulbs to light-emitting diode LED lights. These lights can be used everywhere such as in traffic signals, home lighting and amazingly even in eyelashes and bionic contact lenses. LED lights have an extremely long life span about 50 000 hours and use much less energy than incandescent bulbs. Switching to LED lighting can save a great deal 40 to 70 per cent. LED was invented by Nick Holonyak, Jr born 1928 while working as a consulting scientist at General Electric Company GEC. Holonyak said in *Reader's Digest* 1963 that 'His Holonyak's LED would replace Thomas Edison's light bulb.'

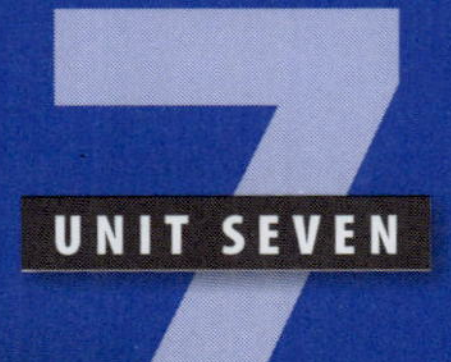

UNIT SEVEN

Aesop's Fables

Focus

Complex sentences; conjunctions; pronouns; commas (5)

Grammar in use

'The Lion and the Mouse' from *Aesop's Fables*

A lion was once awakened by a mouse and he became very angry. **He was about to kill him, when the mouse wretchedly fell down.** The mouse pleaded '**If you would only spare my life, I would be sure to repay your kindness and I would serve you one day.**' The lion laughed and let him go. It happened shortly after this that the lion was caught by a group of men. **They were hunters, who bound him with strong ropes to the ground**. He thought, '**I must get free from these ropes that hold me down.**' **The mouse, who recognised his roar, came and gnawed the rope with his teeth.** As he set him free, the mouse exclaimed '**When we first met, you ridiculed the idea of my ever being able to help you. As I am so small and insignificant, you never expected to receive from me any repayment of your favour.** I now know that it is possible for even a little mouse to assist a mighty lion.'

About grammar

- **Complex sentences** are used to communicate ideas that are too complex for simple or compound sentences.
- A **complex sentence** contains an **independent** main clause that contains the main piece of information and can stand alone as a sentence, and one or more **dependent** (or subordinate) clauses which contain **extra information**; for example, **He was about to kill him**, (independent) **when the mouse wretchedly fell down**. (dependent)
- A **compound-complex sentence** is made from **two** independent clauses and **one or more** dependent clauses; for example, **If you would only spare my life** (dependent), **I would be sure to repay your kindness** (independent) **and I would serve you one day** (independent).
- There are two main types of **dependent** (subordinate) **clauses:** adverbial and relative (or adjectival) clauses.
- **Adverbial clauses** add information about the **verb** in the main clause. They are joined to the main (independent) clause with **subordinating conjunctions**, such as *when, where, as, if, although, while, since, until, whenever, because* and *unless*; for example, **When** *we first met, you ridiculed the idea of my ever being able to help you.* **As** *I am so small and insignificant, you never expected to receive from me any repayment of your favour.*
- Adverbial clauses give information about **time** (*when, before, after, since, while, as, until*), **reason** (*because, since, as*), **purpose** (*in order to, so that*), **place** (*where, wherever*), **manner** (*as, like, the way*), **concession** (*although, though, while*) and **result** (*so that*).

- **Relative clauses** (also known as **adjectival clauses**) provide further information about the **noun** in the main clause. They are joined to the independent clause using **relative pronouns** *that, which, who, whom* and *whose*; for example, *I must get free from these ropes* **that** *hold me down; They were hunters,* **who** *bound him with strong ropes to the ground.*
- **Relative clauses** can be **defining** and **non-defining**.
- A **defining relative clause** identifies or classifies a noun in a **meaningful** way; for example, *Do you know the mouse who helped the lion?* If the relative clause is left out, the sentence feels incomplete—*Do you know the mouse?* (which mouse?)
- A **non-defining relative clause** adds extra **non-essential** information about a noun; for example, *The lion was saved by a group of men, who were hunters.* If the relative clause *who were hunters* is left out, the sentence still makes sense.
- Relative clauses should be **close to the nouns** they relate to, otherwise your message may become confusing and ambiguous; for example, in the following sentences the placement of the relative clause *which are small* influences the meaning of the sentence overall: *Mice,* **which are small**, *are known for having sharp teeth. Mice are known for having sharp teeth,* **which are small**.

1 Underline the **dependent clauses** in these sentences. There may be more than one.

a There are many fables attributed to Aesop that couldn't possibly be his own.

b The legend tells it that Aesop lived during the sixth century BC and scholars have narrowed down his birthplace to a few different places, although no one knows for sure.

c Croesus of Lydia, while king, offered Aesop residency and a job at his court.

d Aesop's favourite stories to tell were fables because they were short.

e Aesop became discouraged because the people were not appreciative enough of the gift that was given to them by King Croesus.

2 Mark the following sentences as **compound**, **complex**, or **compound-complex** (two independent and one or more dependent clauses).

a The bride offended her husband and she had to return home. ____________

b There was a long-established Greek trading colony in Egypt when the stories first appeared.

____

c The mouse gnaws the lion free because the lion is caught in a trap. ____________

d Anthropomorphism features animals with human capabilities and is the common thread throughout Aesop's fables. ____________

e Although the fable is frequently a subject of children's literature, Jerry Pinkney's *The Lion & the Mouse* tells it through pictures alone and won the 2010 Caldecott Medal for its illustrations.

____

3 Choose one of the following **conjunctions** to link the **main** and **dependent** clauses in these sentences. Each conjunction should only be used once.

until   although   if   whenever   while

a ____________ humans and animals share similar traits, humans are different due to their power of reason.

b ____________ fables remain a popular choice for the moral education of children today, some people question their relevance.

c Aesop was revered for his abilities, ____________ it became evident that many of his fables were actually written by others.

d ________________ young readers engage with the story's characters and morals, they really have a chance to learn about human behaviour.

e ________________ the stories highlight poor human decisions and behaviours, they send a message to the reader about the right way to live.

4 Write an **adverbial clause** in the space to complete each sentence. There are many possible answers. Then circle the **verb** in the independent clause to which the adverbial clause adds information. You may use *when, where, as, although, while, since, until, whenever, because, before, after, unless, if* or other conjunctions.

For example: When you read *Aesop's Fables*, (think) about the moral being taught.

a ________________________________, I had never read any of *Aesop's Fables*.

b *Aesop's Fables* is important to read, ________________________________.

c ________________________________, you might learn something of importance.

d ________________________________, I always feel interested.

e ________________________________, I always wonder what happens next.

5 Underline the **relative clause** in each sentence. Write whether it is **defining** (essential) or **non-defining** (non-essential).

a Fables that were written by Aesop usually feature speaking animals. ________________

b *Aesop's Fables*, which was translated into Latin in the 13th century, has been translated into many languages. ________________

c Among the Classical authors who studied Aesop was the Roman poet Horace.

____

d Fables were popular in 17th-century France through the work of Jean de La Fontaine, whose theme was human vanity. ________________

e In a particular fable, a fox and an ape discover the reality that life is no better in the city than in the country. ________________

6 Each of the following sentences has a **relative clause** that needs to be properly placed. Write the sentences with the relative clause in the correct place.

a Aesop spent much of his life living in Greece/who may have been born in Ethiopia/at the court of King Croesus

____

b Fables often pass into our culture as myths/that are used to teach children morals/and legends

____

c The medieval fable/was a lengthy animal story/that contained a hero

____

d A gardener gives it to him as a reward/who offers Aesop a basket of vegetables

____

e Aesop is known for stories that are all fairly short/whose fables provide great entertainment

____

7 Number the following **dependent** and **independent** clauses in the order necessary to create meaningful complex sentences.

a ______ they also allow readers to engage the characters and morals of adulthood
______ unless the reader is very young
______ while the stories describe the challenges of adulthood

b ______ whose stories of clever animals and foolish humans are considered Western civilisation's first morality tales
______ although many know of his fables
______ little is known about the ancient Greek writer Aesop

c ______ which is surprising
______ some scholars believe that he may have been Ethiopian in origin
______ as Aesop's name is unusual

8 The following is a student's English report on **fables**. Rewrite it in order to combine the short simple sentences into longer sentences. There is more than one way to do this.

> Fables are short stories. Fables illustrate a particular moral and teach a lesson to children. Fables often feature animals. They act and talk like humans. They retain their animal characteristics. *Aesop's Fables* are very entertaining. They are short. They keep children's attention. They feature familiar animals. *Aesop's Fables* have been around a long time. They are still popular.

____

____

____

____

Punctuation in use

Fables are a literary genre. **Fables, which may be prose or verse, are short fictional stories** that feature anthropomorphised inanimate objects or forces of nature. This means that these objects and forces are given human qualities such as the ability to talk. **Fables that feature animals and plants are often mythical in nature.** Fables often also present a moral lesson. **While fables are sometimes referred to as parables, this is incorrect.** Parables *do not* feature animals, plants, inanimate objects, or forces of nature that exhibit human qualities.

About punctuation

- We first looked at using **commas** in long sentences in Unit 4. Because **complex sentences** can be long, they often need commas to separate ideas.
- Commas are used to **separate adverbial clauses** at the start of sentences; for example, **While fables are sometimes referred to as parables, this is incorrect.** We sometimes add a comma **after** an independent clause and **before** an adverbial clause, especially where the sentence is long or there is a need to make the sense clearer. For example, *Fables often pass into our culture as myths and legends, since they are used to teach children morals.*

- Commas are also used to **mark a dependent clause** within a sentence, when that clause adds extra but non-essential information. All **non-defining relative clauses** usually have a comma in front of them and a comma after them when they occur **within** a sentence; for example, *Fables,* **which may be prose or verse,** *are short fictional stories.*
- Commas are **never** used in front of a **defining relative clause**; for example, **Fables that feature animals and plants are often mythical in nature.**

1 Use **commas** to separate the **adverbial clauses** at the start of these sentences.

- **a** Unless you plan on reading that book on holiday you shouldn't borrow it.
- **b** When the school bell rang the students left the classroom.
- **c** After you have finished reading the novel your assignment is to write a report.
- **d** While some people prefer to read non-fiction others enjoy fiction and narratives.
- **e** Since we have started learning about fables we will also be exploring parables.

2 Underline the **non-defining** clause and then use **commas** to enclose it. Read the sentences out loud to get a feel for where to place the commas.

- **a** A fable which is a story meant to teach a moral lesson is a type of fictional narrative.
- **b** The characters in a fable who we like to read about are usually animals.
- **c** The name Aesop which means Ethiopia is derived from the Greek word *Aethiop*.
- **d** Aesop who many believe lived on a Greek island called Samos was a slave.
- **e** Parables or allegories where a moral is usually added can be seen in most of Aesop's stories.

3 Place **commas**, if they are needed, around the following **defining and non-defining relative** clauses. Read the sentences out loud to get a feel for where to place the commas.

- **a** Some of the best-known fables that are still read to children today are those attributed to Aesop.
- **b** Many of the fables which include a moral are well known today.
- **c** William Caxton who was a translator first printed *Aesop's Fables* in English in 1484.
- **d** A popular fable that is modern is George Orwell's *Animal Farm*.
- **e** Fables which focused on exposing human weaknesses became popular in 17th-century France.

4 Place **commas** where necessary in the following passage about Aesop. You should use all your knowledge of comma rules.

> Aesop who is credited with the authorship of fables was a slave. Many believed he lived in Samos which is a Greek island in the eastern Aegean Sea but others say he came from Ethiopia. One tradition holds that he came from Thrace while a later one claims he is Phrygian. The name of his first owner was Xanthus who was a philosopher although it is believed that Aesop was eventually freed. Generally speaking many of his fables are characterised by animals and inanimate objects that speak solve problems and who generally have human characteristics.

UNIT EIGHT

Chinese goldminers in Australia

Focus

Prepositions and prepositional phrases; direct speech

Grammar in use

The discovery of gold in New South Wales from the early 1850s saw **a huge influx of migrants in search of instant wealth. The primary result of the Gold Rush was seen in the booming economy** and, for a short time, **gold surpassed wool as the colony's primary export.**

Many of the people who came in search of gold were Chinese men. Drawn from their home villages by the first gold rushes in Victoria, California and New South Wales in the 1850s, **Chinese men began arriving in Australia** in organised groups of 30 to 100 men. **In 1861 there were about 13 000 Chinese in New South Wales, with the majority on the goldfields. Throughout the 19th century, Chinese arrivals continued to the mining regions of New South Wales**, replacing those who had returned home or left for opportunities elsewhere.

The environment would remain hostile to Chinese immigration for years; however, **many remained in Australia**. They would help create the foundations for a strong Chinese–Australian community.

Adapted from
http://www.migrationheritage.nsw.gov.au/exhibition/objectsthroughtime/wong-shop-wagon/
Courtesy of Museum of Applied Arts and Sciences, Sydney

About grammar

- **Prepositions** are words, such as *for, within, on, along, around, by, with, from, to, of, towards, after, beside, into* and *beyond,* that allow you to add detail about **nouns** and **verbs** in a sentence; for example, *The discovery* **of** *gold* **in** *New South Wales* **from** *the early 1850s ...* Some prepositions consist of more than one word; for example, *according to, in between, on top of* and *ahead of.*
- A preposition is generally followed by a **noun, pronoun** or **noun group** to make a prepositional phrase. A **prepositional phrase** allows you to **add details** about the circumstances of an event or situation, or about the people and things involved in them; for example, *The primary result* **of the Gold Rush** *was seen* **in the booming economy**.
- A prepositional **phrase** differs from a clause in that it **does not** contain a subject and a verb. It does, however, have an **object;** for example, in the phrase **in Australia,** *Australia* is the object of the preposition *in.*
- **Prepositional phrases** are an important part of our language because of the way they allow us to build content into a sentence. They allow us to provide more information about:
  - **nouns** or **pronouns**; for example, *a huge influx* **of migrants** *in search* **of instant wealth**
  - **verbs;** for example, *Chinese men began arriving* **in Australia** and *many remained* **in Australia.**

- As shown in the examples above, prepositional phrases act like **adjectives** and **adverbs**. Because of this we sometimes call them **adjectival phrases** (if they add detail about a noun) or **adverbial phrases** (if they add detail about a verb).
- A sentence may contain **more than one** prepositional phrase; for example, *Chinese arrivals continued* **to the mining regions of New South Wales** and *The environment would remain hostile* **to Chinese immigration for years.**
- In general, a prepositional phrase **immediately follows the noun or verb** it relates to; for example, *gold surpassed wool* **as the colony's primary export.**
- However, it can be placed elsewhere for emphasis, especially at the beginning of a clause in front of the subject; for example, **Against the odds**, *some new arrivals slowly impressed themselves upon Sydneysiders*. This is often used for effect in **narratives**. It is also used to make a clearer link between two sentences. *In 1861 there were about 13 000 Chinese in New South Wales, with the majority on the goldfields.* **Throughout the 19th century**, *Chinese arrivals continued to the mining regions of New South Wales …*

Boost your grammar skills

1 Underline the prepositional phrase, then draw a line to the noun or verb it relates to and circle that. There may be more than one phrase.

For example: They (are singing) in a loud voice.

- **a** He reached the goldfields across the paddock in time for work.
- **b** He got a job for his friend from school.
- **c** I will meet him at the mines at lunchtime instead of at home.
- **d** You need to see the man with the blue shirt with regard to work.
- **e** The workers on the minefields took breaks by the creek.
- **f** The men feel sore from digging in the ground along the ridge.

2 Underline the **prepositional phrases** in the sentences below. There may be more than one in each sentence.

- **a** Chinese miners used different mining methods to the Europeans.
- **b** Chinese workers usually operated as a group and they didn't mix with the general population of the goldfields.
- **c** Seven thousand Chinese people came to work at the Araluen gold fields in southern NSW.
- **d** Chinese miners often worked in groups of 30 to 100 men under the direction of a leader.
- **e** Conflict stemmed from resentment of Chinese successes on the goldfields.
- **f** They found gold missed by Caucasian miners in their haste.

3 Choose a preposition to complete the **prepositional phrases** in each of the following sentences.

- **a** The Chinese are said to have rarely worked ________ new areas, preferring to go ________ areas discarded ________ the Europeans.
- **b** Some Chinese felt duty-bound to seek a better future ________ their families who remained ________ home ________ China.

- **c** Most Chinese men wore their hair ________ the form ________ a pigtail which, together ________ their unique clothes and manner ________ travelling, often drew contempt ________ Europeans.
- **d** ________ the early days ________ Chinese settlement in Victoria the centre ________ the Chinese community was ________ the goldfields.
- **e** Most ________ the early Chinese immigrants wanted to return ________ the land ________ their ancestors and later many did.

4 Identify whether each underlined **prepositional phrase** adds information about a **noun** or about a **verb**.

- **a** When gold was discovered <u>in Australia</u>, Chinese immigration significantly increased. ________
- **b** The highest number of arrivals <u>in any one year</u> was 12 396 in 1856. ________
- **c** Racial hostility led to riots <u>on the Buckland goldfields</u> in Victoria in 1857. ________
- **d** Resentment of the Chinese and periodic attacks <u>upon them</u> placed pressure upon the government. ________
- **e** To help them adjust to life <u>in a new land</u>, most Chinese miners joined a society <u>of people from their home districts in China</u>. ________ and ________

5 Underline the **prepositional phrases** in the sentences below that can be moved to the beginning of the clause, in front of the subject. You must choose which prepositional phrase to move so that the sentences still make sense or make better sense.

For example:

Australia developed socially and economically according to historical documents.

Australia developed socially and economically <u>according to historical documents.</u>

- **a** The gold rush in Australia had a significant impact on the formation of the Australian identity.
- **b** The diggers' rebelliousness and contempt for those in charge during this time remains a central theme in any discussion of our history.
- **c** Edward Hargraves discovered a 'grain of gold' in a waterhole near Bathurst and became a legend.
- **d** There was a dramatic change as a result of the discovery within Australian society.

6 Each sentence below is missing the **prepositional phrase** in blue. Mark the best place to put each phrase with a cross (**✗**). There may be more than one possible position.

a	Only a small minority of Chinese people were able to pay for their own voyage and migrate	**to Australia free of debt**
b	They were often forced to move or made to work on empty sites	**to new areas**
c	The government tried to award basic rights and provided them with improved legal access	**to the Chinese**
d	Many Chinese migrants left the colony or returned to China	**for other states**
e	It was common for Chinese to be removed where gold had been discovered	**from areas**

7 Underline all the **prepositional phrases** in the following short text. Take note of the way these phrases have allowed the writer to 'pack' so much information into the paragraph.

> The Chinese diggers moved from goldfield to goldfield within NSW and across the border. Their presence and experience are shown from the observations of Anglo-Australians, from archaeological digs and from objects saved by families and community members. There are few written accounts and sources from a Chinese perspective. The Chinese attracted particular attention and local newspapers were quick to comment on their diligence, tirelessness and productivity. Admiration of their work ethic was offset by envy and resentment.
>
> Adapted from
> http://www.migrationheritage.nsw.gov.au/exhibition/objectsthroughtime/wong-shop-wagon

Punctuation in use

European miners were angered by an increasing Chinese presence in the fields, and as a result Chinese diggers were subject to growing resentment. **'A general and unanimous rising should take place for the purpose of driving the Chinese off the goldfield,' declared an angry group** of European and American miners in Bendigo in 1854. Colonial authorities attempted to control the violence.

In 1855, a member of the Castlemaine bench intervened. **'All men here are equal,' he declared. 'They come here from all parts of the world in equality, and you have no right to drive any away because they do not work as you please!'** However, in 1857 a series of violent clashes occurred between Chinese and white miners at the Buckland River goldfield in Victoria.

Adapted from http://www.sbs.com.au/gold/story.php?storyid=56 by the Victorian Cultural Collaboration (VCC) © SBS

About punctuation

- **Direct speech** refers to actual words spoken by a person. You may be familiar with the use of direct speech in narrative and other imaginative writing, but you need to be aware of its usefulness in more formal informative writing such as essays and reports. It is useful in this kind of writing to use the actual words spoken or written by another person in order to make your points.
- Direct speech is enclosed by quotation marks (also called inverted commas). **Quotation marks** can be single (' ') or double (" ") for **direct speech**, as long as they are the **same** throughout the text.
- The **ending punctuation**, including full stops, question marks and exclamation marks, should be enclosed in the quotation marks; for example, **'They come here from all parts of the world in equality, and you have no right to drive any away because they do not work as you please!'** (The exclamation mark is enclosed.)
- However, if the direct speech ends in a full stop but is followed by words such as *he said* or *announced,* a **comma** is used instead of a full stop; for example, **'A general and unanimous rising should take place for the purpose of driving the Chinese off the goldfield,' declared an angry group.**

- When two sentences in direct speech are **interrupted** by information that is not part of the quote, the inverted commas are closed after the first sentence, and new ones are opened to continue the second quoted sentence; for example, *'All men here are equal,'* **he declared.** *'They come here from all parts of the world in equality, and you have no right to drive any away because they do not work as you please.'*
- However, when the quoted sentence is **split** and the sentence is **not finished**, a comma is placed **after** the first section of quoted speech, and a comma is **also** placed **after** the speaking clause; for example, *'All men are equal,' the member shouted, 'and you have no right to send anyone away!'* These sentence breaks should be placed at a point in the sentence where they make sense.
- If the quote consists of **more than one paragraph**, quotation marks should be placed at the **beginning of each paragraph** and also at the **end of the quote**.

Boost your punctuation skills

1 Punctuate the **direct speech** in the sentences below using **quotation marks** and the correct **ending punctuation**.

- **a** There is no doubt that the gold rushes had a huge effect on our development as a nation said the teacher.
- **b** Do you know where the first grain of gold was discovered? asked Kamal.
- **c** You must make sure you visit Ballarat when you drive through Victoria! insisted Mrs Morrison.
- **d** Hargraves said: The similarity in geological features between the Australian and Californian goldfields boded well for the search of gold in Australia.
- **e** There has been a universal rush to the diggings the commissioner stated.

2 Place missing **end punctuation** in the following examples of **direct speech**.

- **a** 'Did you know that the 1850s also saw the construction of the first railway ______' Maria said.
- **b** 'Why would the new convict arrivals want to work for a living when a fortune awaited them on the goldfields ______' asked our history teacher.
- **c** 'We swear by the Southern Cross to stand truly by each other, and fight to defend our rights and liberties ______' said miners at the Eureka Stockade.
- **d** 'Eureka ______' shouted the miner as he struck a pocket of gold.
- **e** 'Modern ideas about goldfield life ignore the filth, greed, crime, selfishness and racism that were actually very common ______' stated the historian.

3 Correctly place missing **quotation marks, commas** and **ending punctuation** in the following sentences.

- **a** When finds of wondrous treasure set all the south ablaze wrote Henry Lawson and you and I were faithful mates all through the roaring days
- **b** Today I learnt that 40000 Chinese made their way to Australia said Tobias In 1861, Chinese immigrants made up 3.3 per cent of the Australian population

c The gold rush brought to Australia people with a range of skills and professions said the lecturer and this was unthought-of prior to the discovery of gold.

d Life was difficult for the Chinese in Australia explained the historian In exchange for their passage money, they worked on the goldfields until their debt was paid off.

4 Rewrite the following indirect questions as **direct speech**. You need to consider which words are actually spoken. You may also need to change the tense of the verb and change or add a word.

a The authorities said that the Chinese were known as untiring workers and that's why there was so much jealousy.

____

____

____

b The students wanted to know why nobody stepped in to help the Chinese goldminers during the attack.

____

____

____

c I told my friends about how shocked I was at the violence exhibited towards Asian goldminers!

____

____

____

5 Correctly insert **quotation marks** and **ending punctuation** in the following text.

Lum Khen Yang was a Chinese goldminer who later became a successful merchant in Melbourne. Here he describes the situation in China that led to his decision to come to Australia:

Our money and property were plundered said Lum Khen Yang. We had not the means of purchasing a morsel to put into our mouths and there appeared no way by which we could extricate ourselves from poverty. Yang continued: But then we heard intelligence regarding a new goldfield in an English colony.

We were told that men from all parts of the world were congregated there Yang explained that the people were peaceably disposed, and that the country abounded in everything.

The idea of going to such a country was delightful! he exclaimed.

Adapted from Lum Khen Yang in *The Wesleyan Chronicle*, 1 February 1859 quoted in *Colonial Casualties: Chinese in Early Victoria*, Melbourne University Press, Melbourne, Vic. http://ergo.slv.vic.gov.au/explore-history/golden-victoria/life-fields/chinese

UNIT NINE

Social learning

Focus

Active and passive voice; possessive apostrophes

Grammar in use

Extract from a report on social learning in schools

All schools **are responsible** for promoting social and emotional skills in their students. Every day, in varied and creative ways, schools and their teachers **work** together to develop understanding, strategies and skills that promote their students' self-worth. However, some schools **have developed** specific programs to do this.

This state-wide project **was carried out** to show the positive benefits targeted social-awareness programs can have for school-aged students. The outcomes in the report are based on observations of students in schools where a social-learning program **has been implemented**.

About grammar

Active and passive voice

- **Verbs** can be in the **active** or **passive** voice. The **active** voice (e.g. *he wrote, we understood*) is the more usual form of the verb but the **passive** voice (e.g. *it was written, it was understood*) is also useful to express our ideas effectively.
- We use the **active voice** when we want to focus on the person or thing **doing the action** (verb). We make that person or thing the subject of the sentence; for example, in all three sentences below the focus is on the schools (because 'schools' is the subject).

  All schools **are responsible** *for promoting social and emotional skills …*
  … schools and their teachers **work** *together…*
  … some schools **have developed** *specific programs …*
- The **active voice** is used more than the passive in **narratives** and **recounts** because it is more direct and focuses on the people being written about; for example, The *small boy* **addressed** *the class. He* **spoke** *in a loud, clear voice.*
- We use the **passive voice** when we want to focus on the person or thing **being acted upon**, or on the **process** or **action itself**, rather than the people doing the action. We make that person or thing the **subject** of the sentence; for example, *This state-wide project* **was carried out** … (The focus is on the project, and it is not important to talk about the individuals who carried it out.)
- The passive voice is useful when we don't want or need to mention the person or thing completing the action. This may be because it is obvious who or what they are, or because it is not important to say who they are; for example, … *a social-learning program* **has been implemented**. (The focus is on the program and the implementation; it is not important to say who implemented them.)

- The **passive voice** is used more often in **essays, reports** and other **formal** writing because it focuses on processes rather than specific people and things. **Repeated** or **inappropriate use** of the **passive voice** may result in texts that are difficult to read. The writing becomes dominated by **things** and **concepts** instead of people and it is easy to lose a feeling for who or what is doing the action.
- While it is often necessary and accepted to switch between active and passive voice when writing, **within sentences** try to maintain either a passive or active voice.

Boost your grammar skills

1 Mark each of the following sentences either *A* for **active** or *P* for **passive**.

a The teacher observed at least five students every day. ______

b The students were closely observed by their teacher. ______

c Reports are constantly being written on this topic. ______

d Twenty teachers are writing reports on this important topic. ______

e At the end of the term, the teacher wrote about one significant incident. ______

f All playground incidents are written up by teachers on duty. ______

2 Rewrite each **passive** sentence in the **active** voice so that the focus is on the person or thing, **not** the process. You may need to change the verb's tense.

For example: The report was generated by five local schools.
Five local schools generated the report.

a The young adult group was established by young people.

____

b The results will be revealed by the Principal next Friday.

____

c The equipment was manufactured by a company in China.

____

d New skills can be learnt by socially isolated young adults.

____

e Real-life experiences are presented throughout the program by team leaders.

____

3 Underline the **verbs** in the following sentences and write *active* or *passive* beside each.

For example: Students learn important social skills. active

a Teenagers can build on their creative ideas through discussion. ______________

b Relationships are strengthened by people who care. ______________

c Recognising emotions is considered important by health professionals. ______________

d Students learn that negotiation is necessary in relationships. ______________

e Negotiation is judged as necessary for success in relationships. ______________

4 In each sentence below, underline the person or thing completing the action (the **actor**). If the actor is not named, write *NA* after the sentence.

For example: Knowledge is gained by students in the course.

- **a** Positive learning is achieved by teenagers who are challenged and engaged.
- **b** Improved social and emotional skills will be achieved by the end of the session.
- **c** Community involvement is generally recognised as having positive effects.
- **d** Self-discipline is considered necessary for success by all teachers.
- **e** Technology is considered a major influence on young people.

5 Tick (✔) the sentences that use **active** voice **consistently.** Cross (✘) those that don't.

- **a** Self-development leads to improved self-confidence and promotes mental health.
- **b** Students develop independent opinions and a sense of accomplishment is experienced.
- **c** Young people have to work through a broad range of issues and they may have to deal with changes to their feelings.
- **d** Mature relationships encourage lifelong friendships and an appreciation of home and family is promoted.

6 Tick (✔) the sentences that use the **passive** voice **consistently**. Cross (✘) those that don't.

- **a** Past research has identified parental influence on self-esteem but equal attention has not been given to the important effect of friends.
- **b** A sense of self is formed through family, and the home environment is considered very important.
- **c** A sense of belonging is instilled by many positive factors but children tend to develop self-esteem early in childhood.
- **d** The signs of high and low self-esteem are often monitored at schools and teachers have the power to affect a student's self-esteem.

7 The following text uses both the active and passive voice. Using the **base verb** that has been provided, decide if the **active or passive** form of the verb is needed in each space.

> Social awareness (involve) ________________ two key areas. Firstly, it is an awareness that social problems (face) ________________ regularly by individuals and communities. Secondly, it (to be) ________________ the ability to sympathise with an individual's thoughts and feelings and to realise that individuals (impact) ________________ by wider forces within their community. Social awareness (promote) ________________ respectful relationships and encourages skills that (create)________________ by emotions and responsible decision-making.

Punctuation in use

> Positive development of **the social and emotional skills of all citizens** is critical to society. **A person's success** may depend upon it.
>
> Risky behaviours, including drug use, violence, bullying and dropping out, can be prevented or reduced when efforts are made to develop **students' social and emotional skills**.
>
> Learning is a social process that takes place in collaboration with **an individual's teachers**, peers and family. Instruction is best achieved in the classroom, although parents' involvement in supporting **their children's development** is also necessary.

About punctuation

- **Apostrophes** are used to show **possession** of one noun or noun group by another; for example, **A person's success** → *the success of a person.*
- Apostrophes of possession are always placed **after the last letter** of the possessing noun. Asking the question 'Who does the owning?' will help you decide where the apostrophe should be placed.
- For **singular** possessing nouns, the apostrophe is placed **before the *s***; for example, **an individual's teachers** (the teachers of the individual). Singular nouns which end in *s* are treated in the same way; for example, *The class's teacher.*
- For **plural** possessing nouns, the apostrophe is placed **after the *s***; for example, **students' social and emotional skills** (the social and emotional skills of the students).
- When the possessing noun is **irregular**, as in *women, men, children, teeth* or *mice* the apostrophe is placed **before the *s***; for example, **their children's development** (development of the children).
- Sometimes, especially with **plural** possessing nouns, it is better to avoid the apostrophe construction and use ***of*** instead; for example; **the social and emotional skills of all citizens** sounds better than *all citizens' social and emotional skills.*
- **Possessive pronouns** do **not** need apostrophes; for example, *ours, theirs, yours, hers, its* and *his.*
- **Not all words that end in *s* take an apostrophe**—only those that 'possess' the following noun; for example, *The parents were invited to participate* (no apostrophe is needed in *parents*, which is a simple plural); *The parents' participation was essential* (an apostrophe is needed to show possession).
- When **two named people** own something, you only need to put the apostrophe after the second name; for example, *Joe and Rosie's school* (**not** 'Joe's and Rosie's school').

Boost your punctuation skills

1 Circle the alternative that uses the **apostrophe of possession** correctly.

a Teachers'/Teacher's prior backgrounds and experiences are drawn on to improve each student's/students' experiences.

b Being challenged to question one's/ones' own personal values is never easy.

c Self-awareness influences people's/peoples' personalities, value systems and beliefs.

d Learner's/Learners' needs are met when they adopt a reflective approach.

e Student's/Students' ability to understand and discuss their own needs influences a teacher's/teachers' flexibility to adjust lessons.

2 Tick (✔) the sentences that have used **apostrophes** correctly and rewrite the other sentences, using correct punctuation, on the lines below.

- **a** Louisa's and Antonio's teacher is teaching them about Maslow's hierarchy.
- **b** In Maslow's hierarchy of needs the step before self-actualisation is self-esteem.
- **c** Maslow took the position that a persons' competence is directly affected by the view they take of themselves.
- **d** One's self-esteem relies on factors like responsibility and accountability.
- **e** An individual's self-worth, when based on external factors, is more likely to be unhealthy.
- **f** The book on the topic was hers'—I placed it on your desk.

____

____

____

____

____

____

3 Place missing **apostrophes** in the following sentences.

- **a** Marisas list of accomplishments helped her to build a sense of self-worth.
- **b** Fiona and Charles list of accomplishments included having a sense of humour.
- **c** Friends who value you are important and a friends acceptance is invaluable.
- **d** Adolescents feelings of belonging are affected when they try too hard to fit in.
- **e** Once you see the childs self-image begin to improve, you will see significant gains in achievement.
- **f** Adolescence causes stress on teenagers bodies, minds and emotions.
- **g** Emotional well-being is influenced by a persons ability to relate to other people.
- **h** Self-esteem can be influenced by peoples individual achievements.

4 Place **apostrophes** where necessary in the following recount.

> In class today we discussed self-awareness. Everyones feelings, behaviours and characteristics were discussed. We all agreed with Alyssa and Kierans idea that people who are self-aware tend to make wiser decisions. The whole class ideas were written on the board by Mr Pugh, while Yukiko typed up the notes on Thans laptop. He's been kind enough to let us use his laptop all term. We discussed how peoples self-awareness may allow them to develop deeper relationships since they're more likely to understand what they want or need. Our class was really interesting.

UNIT TEN

10 Virginia Woolf

Focus
Common sentence errors; full stop and comma errors

Grammar in use

Text A

Note: this text includes errors.

***A Haunted House* is a short story** written by Virginia Woolf **it tells about a ghost couple who occupy the same dwelling as a living couple. The living couple are the current occupants of a house the ghost couple are the past occupants of the house.** In her story Woolf raises hope about this life and about the afterlife. **Presenting an optimistic vision of human relationships. The story is about the treasure of love, it is about rediscovery.** The tone is playful and light-hearted and so the reader realises that the ghosts are no threat to the living couple.

Text B

From *A Haunted House* by Virginia Woolf

The wind roars up the avenue. Trees stoop and bend this way and that. Moonbeams splash and spill wildly in the rain. **But the beam of the lamp falls straight from the window.** The candle burns stiff and still. Wandering through the house, opening the windows, whispering not to wake us, the ghostly couple seek their joy.

'Here we slept,' she says. And he adds, **'Kisses without number.' 'Waking in the morning—' 'Silver between the trees—'** 'Upstairs—' **'In the garden—' 'When summer came—' 'In winter snowtime—'** The doors go shutting far in the distance, gently knocking like the pulse of a heart.

About grammar

Effective word choice is only one part of expressing ideas clearly; you must also arrange those words in correct and logical sentence patterns.

Both Text A and Text B above contain sentence patterns such as **fragments, run-ons** and **comma splices** which are generally considered to be writing errors. In Text A, which is part of a student essay, these patterns should not appear. Sentence fragments, run-ons and comma splices have **no place** in formal writing such as **essays** and **reports**, where they seriously undermine the effect of your expression.

These patterns are sometimes acceptable in informal personal texts, such as emails, and even in some more formal texts such as newspaper and magazine articles. They are quite often used in **imaginative writing**, as they are in Text B above. In Text B, a novel extract, they are used for their narrative effect and as devices to contribute to the supernatural theme. In general, these sentence patterns are only used by confident writers, and only when they know that the reader is certain to **understand** their **meaning**.

A **sentence fragment** is an **incomplete** sentence. Some fragments are incomplete because they lack either a subject or a verb; for example, in Text B, **'Kisses without number'** (What about the kisses?), **'In the garden—'** (Who or what was in the garden?) and **'Silver between the trees—'** (What about the silver between the trees?). (Note: in this text these fragments work to emphasise the ghostly theme, but they would not always be appropriate.)

Other sentence fragments are **dependent clauses** that make no sense on their own unless a main independent clause is added; for example, **Presenting an optimistic vision of human relationships** in Text A (What exactly is being presented? Who is presenting?). Note: you learnt about dependent clauses in Unit 7.

The most common **types** of **sentence fragments** are:

- **adverbial clauses** beginning with **subordinating conjunctions**, such as *when, where, as, if, although, while, since, until, whenever, because* and *unless*; for example, **When summer came**; *Although the candle burns*
- **relative clauses** beginning with **relative pronouns** *that, which, who, whom* and *whose*; for example, *That stoop and bend; Who whispered softly*
- **prepositional phrases**; for example, **In the garden**; **In winter snowtime**
- ***ing* clauses**; for example, **Waking in the morning** and **Presenting an optimistic vision of human relationships**
- **clauses beginning with coordinating conjunctions** *and, but, for, nor, or, so* and *yet*; for example, **But the beam of the lamp falls straight from the window**.

A **run-on** is when two independent clauses are joined together in one sentence without being properly separated. A full stop or coordinating conjunction is needed to connect the independent clauses.

For example, **The living couple are the current occupants of a house the ghost couple are the past occupants of the house**.

↓

The living couple are the current occupants of a house. The ghost couple are the past occupants of the house.
The living couple are the current occupants of a house and the ghost couple are the past occupants of the house.

Sometimes you can fix a run-on by adding a **relative pronoun**.

For example, A Haunted House *is a short story it tells about a ghost couple who occupy the same dwelling as a living couple.*

↓

A Haunted House *is a short story* **which** *tells about a ghost couple who occupy the same dwelling as a living couple.*

A **comma splice** is similar to a run-on but it occurs when two independent clauses are joined only by a **comma**. Again, a coordinating conjunction or a full stop is needed between the two clauses.

For example, **The story is about the treasure of love, it is about rediscovery.**

↓

The story is about the treasure of love. It is about rediscovery.
The story is about the treasure of love, but it is also about rediscovery.

Using **punctuation** to avoid run-ons and comma splices is explored at the end of this unit.

Boost your grammar skills

1 Write *S* for **sentence** or *F* for **fragment** besides each of the following.

a That pulses and moves. ______

b They arrived that afternoon. ______

c The candle burns stiff. ______

d While the moon shone. ______

e Whispering not to wake us. ______

f Moonbeams splash and spill. ______

g The heart of the house beats. ______

h Where we left our treasure. ______

2 Underline **one** word that should be removed in order to create a **complete sentence**.

a When they look for something in the garden.

b Although Woolf attempts to uncover aspects of human relationships.

c Since love rarely runs a smooth course.

d Because the ghostly lovers' marriage is interrupted by death.

e While Woolf attempts to reveal unspoken aspects of human relationships.

3 Identify each of the following as either *F* for **fragment**, *R* for **run-on**, or *C* for **comma splice**.

a Nearer they come, they stop at the doorway. ______

b A moment later the light faded the sun disappeared. ______

c Or so Woolf believed. ______

d The reader is interested, they want to keep reading. ______

e Which belongs to her. ______

f The house all empty the doors standing open. ______

4 Choose the **correct alternative** for each sentence.

a i They had occupied the house for more than a century before the current residents moved in. First as living creatures and then as ghosts.

ii They had occupied the house for more than a century before the current residents moved in, first as living creatures and then as ghosts.

b i As the ghosts search for their 'treasure', they roam the house and they stop to reminisce.

ii As the ghosts search for their 'treasure', they roam the house, they stop to reminisce.

c i The ghosts spend some time expressing their love for each other and they enjoy a quiet moment together.

ii The ghosts spend some time expressing their love for each other, they enjoy a quiet moment together.

d i After an encounter with the ghost couple in their bedroom, the living couple realise what the ghosts are seeking, they are no longer afraid.

ii After an encounter with the ghost couple in their bedroom, the living couple realise what the ghosts are seeking and they are no longer afraid.

5 Turn each sentence fragment into a **complete sentence**.

For example: Having not read the book
Having not read the book, she decided to give it a try.

a A moment later

______

b Wanting the story to continue

______

c Walking through the room

______

d While I was at the door

______

e Being a keen reader

______

6 Rewrite the following short texts **without any fragments, run-ons or comma splices**. There is more than one way to achieve this.

a A man and woman who occupy a house hear male and female ghosts. Wandering about the dwelling. They talk about finding a treasure.

______

______

b Because love endures in *A Haunted House*. Not even fate keeps the ghostly lovers separated they exist in the afterlife together.

______

______

c Woolf reveals that connections are made between all souls, living and dead, she examines these in great detail.

______

______

d The ghosts had occupied the house more than a century before the current residents, the living couple seem unaware of them. Although they are asleep.

______

______

e After the man died. He joined his ghostly wife at the house they had once occupied this was the same house where the living man and woman now reside.

______

______

7 Below are texts which contain **sentence fragments.** Tick (✔) the texts which have a writing style appropriate for fragments.

a Being an interested student. She enjoys reading mysteries and science-fiction. ______

b In the dark. Walking quietly. Then waiting. Our breath, shallow and fast, betrayed our anxiety. ______

c How are you? All good here. Having a get-together on Friday. Hope you can make it. ______

d The author is well-known and considered successful. In literary circles. ______

Punctuation in use

Note: the following text contains punctuation errors.

Virginia Woolf began writing professionally in 1900. When her first novel *The Voyage Out* was published in 1915, Woolf went on to publish novels and essays as a public intellectual, where she received praise from critics. **She is seen as a major twentieth-century novelist she is also regarded as a writer who had very modern ideas**.

Woolf is considered to be a major innovator in the English language. In her works she experimented with stream of consciousness and the psychological as well as emotional motives of characters. **Woolf's reputation fell sharply after World War II, her importance was re-established with the growth of the feminist movement in the 1970s**.

Adapted from https://en.wikipedia.org/wiki/Virginia_Woolf

About punctuation

You already know that **commas and full stops** are used to separate one idea from another to help create meaningful sentences. Using commas and full stops correctly will also help you **avoid** using **run-ons** and **comma splices**.

- As you saw above a **run-on** occurs when two or more sentences are joined together **without full stops** or **coordinating conjunctions** (*for, and, nor, but, or, yet, so*).

  For example, **She is seen as a major twentieth-century novelist she is also regarded as a writer who had very modern ideas**.

  She is seen as a major twentieth-century novelist **and** *she is also regarded as a writer who had very modern ideas.*

  She is seen as a major twentieth-century novelist. She is also regarded as a writer who had very modern ideas.

- When there is a strong connection between the first and second clauses a **semicolon** (;) is a useful way to correct run-ons; for example, *She is seen as a major twentieth-century novelist; she is also regarded as a writer who had very modern ideas.* Semicolons are covered in Unit 13.

- A **comma splice** is where two independent sentences are joined by a **comma**, but actually need a **coordinating conjunction or a full stop**; for example: **Woolf's reputation fell sharply after World War II, her importance was re-established with the growth of the feminist movement in the 1970s**.

  Woolf's reputation fell sharply after World War II **but** *her importance was re-established with the growth of the feminist movement in the 1970s.*

  Woolf's reputation fell sharply after World War II. Her importance was re-established with the growth of the feminist movement in the 1970s.

Boost your punctuation skills

1 Write *S* for **well-structured sentence** and *R* for **run-on**.

a Virginia Woolf's distinctiveness as a fiction writer has concealed her central strength she is considered the major poetic novelist in the English language. ______

b Woolf's fictional worlds are filled with strong auditory and visual impressions. ______

c The intensity of Virginia Woolf's writing improves the ordinary settings of most of her novels. ______

d Her irregular, free-form prose style inspired her peers and earned her much admiration. ______

e Writer Virginia Woolf was born into a privileged English household in 1882 she was raised by free-thinking parents. ______

f Woolf is described as having a hostile relationship with her doctors she is perceived as a woman who had mental health problems. ______

2 Use a **full stop** or **coordinating conjunction** to correct the following run-on sentences.

a Woolf was known for her mood swings she also experienced bouts of deep depression.

______

b Two of Woolf's brothers had been educated at Cambridge all the girls were taught at home and had access to the family's lavish Victorian library.

______

______

c The hormones of early adolescence spun Woolf into a nervous breakdown the death of her mother also deeply affected her.

______

______

d Her sister Vanessa and brother Adrian sold the family home in Hyde Park Gate they then purchased a house in London.

______

e Woolf's novel *Mrs Dalloway* utilises interior monologues as a technique it also highlights themes of feminism and mental illness in post-World War I England.

______

______

3 Circle the **comma splice** in each of the following sentences.

a Despite appearances, she continued to regularly suffer from bouts of depression, she suffered from dramatic mood swings as well.

b Long summer holidays were spent at Talland House in St Ives, Cornwall, this was considered a happy time for her.

c Stella, Virginia's sister, married Jack Hills in 1897, she too died suddenly on her return from her honeymoon.

d In 1921, Virginia's first collection of short stories appeared called *Monday or Tuesday*, most were written using a new style.

e Since about 1908, Virginia had been writing her first novel *The Voyage Out*, it was finished by 1913 but, owing to delays, it was not published until 1915.

4 Re-write the following sentences that contain **run-ons** and **comma splices.** You may use commas, full stops and coordinating conjunctions. There is more than one way to achieve a correct response.

a The effects of bipolar disorder at times caused Woolf to enter therapy, she withdrew from her busy social life she was distressed that she could not focus long enough to read or write.

____

____

b She spent time in nursing homes for rest, she frankly referred to herself as 'mad' she said she heard voices and had visions.

____

____

c Woolf wrote an extraordinary number of diaries, letters, critical reviews, essays, short stories and novels. Woolf's work continues to be the source of much scholarly study, she is still popular today.

____

____

d Woolf's husband was watchful for the onset of the next depression in his wife she would get migraine headaches and lie sleepless at night.

____

____

e Woolf's works examine the difficulties that female writers and intellectuals face, they are relevant today, men are still perceived to hold uneven legal and economic power.

____

____

5 Circle where the **run-ons** and **comma splices** occur in the following paragraph. Write *R* for run-on or *C* for comma splice above each.

> *A Room of One's Own* is an extended essay by Virginia Woolf, it was first published in 1929. The essay was based on a series of lectures she delivered at two women's colleges at Cambridge University in England in 1928 the title of the essay comes from Woolf's perception that '... a woman must have money and a room of her own if she is to write fiction'. Woolf wrote that women have been kept from writing because of their relative poverty, she believed that financial freedom would bring women the freedom to write. The title also refers to any author's right to freedom Woolf strongly believed in an individual's right to be creative. The essay examines whether women are capable of producing work like William Shakespeare it addresses the limitations women writers have faced historically and in the present.
>
> Adapted from https://en.wikipedia.org/wiki/A_Room_of_One%27s_Own

Revision Test 2

Grammar

Shade one circle to show the correct answer.

In questions 1–2, which one is a sentence?

1
- ◯ A tiny pebble got stuck in my shoe.
- ◯ A tiny pebble.
- ◯ A tiny pebble in my shoe.

2
- ◯ Looking towards the future.
- ◯ Brothers and sisters looking.
- ◯ I am looking towards the future.

3 Which is a compound sentence?
- ◯ While celebrating food, the food museum also celebrates cultural influence worldwide.
- ◯ The food museum celebrates food and it celebrates cultural influence worldwide.
- ◯ The food museum celebrates food, cultural influence and history worldwide.

In questions 4–5, insert the correct pronoun in the second clause.

4 There is an immense amount of plastic floating in the world's oceans, and ______ equals the mass of about 38 000 African elephants.

5 Plastics are widely manufactured worldwide but ______ don't easily break down.

In questions 6–7, which is a complex sentence?

6
- ◯ Since beginning to jog every evening, I feel a lot healthier.
- ◯ I jog every evening and I feel a lot healthier.
- ◯ Getting out every evening makes you feel healthier.

7
- ◯ I want to ignore the phone but it keeps ringing.
- ◯ That annoying phone keeps on ringing.
- ◯ I was about to answer the phone when it stopped ringing.

8 Which underlined group of words is an adverbial clause?
- ◯ Before you arrived, _I was preparing dinner_ and thinking about how much I love cooking.
- ◯ _Before you arrived_, I was preparing dinner and thinking about how much I love cooking.
- ◯ Before you arrived, I was preparing dinner and thinking about _how much I love cooking_.

9 Which underlined group of words is a defining clause?
- ◯ Cars _that run on electricity_ are better for the environment since they don't emit fumes.
- ◯ Cars that run on electricity _are better for the environment_ since they don't emit fumes.
- ◯ Cars that run on electricity are better for the environment _since they don't emit fumes._

10 Which underlined group of words is a non-defining clause?

- ◯ The boy, who woke up after 12 years, <u>had been in a coma</u> yet could hear everything being said.
- ◯ The boy, <u>who woke up after 12 years,</u> had been in a coma yet could hear everything being said.
- ◯ The boy, who woke up after 12 years, had been in a coma <u>yet could hear everything being said.</u>

11 Which two circled words are prepositions?

(Within) our lifetime, (we) can expect (great) changes (in) technology.

◯ ◯ ◯ ◯

12 Which of the following is a prepositional phrase?

- ◯ When I saw you
- ◯ After the theatre production
- ◯ Who enjoys swimming and surfing

13 Which underlined word is the prepositional phrase's object?

- ◯ After lunch, I would like a <u>walk</u> and then a rest.
- ◯ After <u>lunch</u>, I would like a walk and then a rest.
- ◯ After lunch, I would like a walk and then a <u>rest</u>.

14 In the following sentence, circle the best place to place the prepositional phrase *in her garden*?

a The old lady who has lived next door **b** for the last 20 years **c** is very well known for the beautiful flowers **d**

15 Which sentence is written in the passive voice?

- ◯ The health reforms were implemented in all hospitals at the beginning of last year.
- ◯ They implemented the health reforms in all hospitals at the beginning of last year.
- ◯ The health reforms began in all hospitals at the beginning of last year.

16 This sentence is written in the active voice: Australian scientists are investigating the effect of plastic trash on sea life.

Which of the sentences below is the passive voice form of the sentence?
Note: you need to keep the same sense and the same tense of the original sentence.

- ◯ The effect of plastic trash on sea life was investigated by Australian scientists
- ◯ The effect of plastic trash on sea life is being investigated by Australian scientists.
- ◯ The effect of plastic trash on sea life was being investigated by Australian scientists.

17 Which of the following is a sentence fragment?

- ◯ I was thinking about how literature has changed over time.
- ◯ Thinking about how literature has changed over time.
- ◯ Thinking about how literature has changed over time is interesting.

18 Which of the following contains a run-on sentence?

- ◯ Climate change has made winters a little bit warmer, and many bird species are now wintering a lot farther north than they did a few decades ago.
- ◯ A new study finds that climate change has made winters a little bit warmer many bird species are now wintering a lot farther north.

19 Which underlined group of words is a sentence fragment?

- ◯ I was walking home. In summer sunshine. It was so lovely, I needed more.
- ◯ I was walking home. In summer sunshine. It was so lovely, I needed more.
- ◯ I was walking home. In summer sunshine. It was so lovely, I needed more.

Punctuation

1 Which sentence uses punctuation correctly?

- ◯ They all decided to go—Sinead, Seana, Isabel and Alex—cycling.
- ◯ All four of them—Sinead, Seana, Isabel, and Alex—decided to go cycling.
- ◯ They all—Sinead, Seana, Isabel, and Alex decided—to go cycling.

2 Which sentence uses punctuation correctly?

- ◯ Hipparchus is known for the discovery of the first recorded nova (a new star).
- ◯ The first recorded (nova) was discovered by an astronomer.
- ◯ The first recorded nova was discovered by a Greek (astronomer) Hipparchus.

3 Brackets have been left out of this sentence. Circle the two places where they should go.

Sustainability is about taking what we need to live now without jeopardising the future. We need to live in a sustainable way this means something should be able to continue forever.

4 Dashes have been left out of this sentence. Circle where they should go.

We are going overseas soon I'm so excited and I'm going to start blogging about it straight away.

5 Which sentence is punctuated correctly?

- ◯ A large proportion of all life, which mostly exists in the ocean is unknown to this day.
- ◯ A large proportion of all life, which mostly exists in the ocean is unknown, to this day.
- ◯ A large proportion of all life, which mostly exists in the ocean, is unknown to this day.

6 Which sentence contains a comma splice?

- ◯ Permaculture is a philosophy of working with nature, it relies on extended and thoughtful observation.
- ◯ Permaculture is a philosophy of working with nature, which relies on extended and thoughtful observation.
- ◯ Permaculture is a philosophy of working with, rather than against nature, and of extended and thoughtful observation.

7 Where would you place a full stop to avoid a run-on in the following sentence?

Permaculture is about growing your own food with green design it works with people, our natural environment and ecosystems.

In questions 8–10, which sentence is correctly punctuated?

8
- ◯ The delegate said, 'We believe every person should enjoy all of the rights stated in the Universal Declaration of Human Rights'!
- ◯ The delegate said, 'We believe every person should enjoy all of the rights stated in the Universal Declaration of Human Rights!'
- ◯ The delegate said 'We believe every person should enjoy all of the rights stated in the Universal Declaration of Human Rights'!

9
- ◯ 'Amnesty International was founded after a group of students in Portugal were jailed for raising a toast to freedom', reported the student.
- ◯ 'Amnesty International was founded after a group of students in Portugal were jailed for raising a toast to freedom,' reported the student.
- ◯ 'Amnesty International was founded after a group of students in Portugal were jailed for raising a toast to freedom' reported the student.

10
- ◯ 'Human rights', argued the lawyer, 'are the basic freedoms and protections that people are entitled to simply because they are human beings.'
- ◯ 'Human rights' argued the lawyer 'are the basic freedoms and protections that people are entitled to simply because they are human beings.'
- ◯ 'Human rights,' argued the lawyer. 'Are the basic freedoms and protections that people are entitled to simply because they are human beings.'

In questions 11–13, which sentence is correct?

11
- ◯ What is your family doing for you're birthday this year?
- ◯ What is it your doing for your birthday this year?
- ◯ What is it you're doing for your birthday this year?

12
- ◯ Peta and James's school is going to have its first swimming carnival there.
- ◯ Peta's and James' school is going to have it's first swimming carnival there.
- ◯ Peta and Jame's school is going to have its first swimming carnival their.

13
- ◯ I didn't want to be the one to show you Janays house, but you wouldve found it anyway. It's next door to Fiona's place.
- ◯ I didn't want to be the one to show you Janay's house, but you would've found it anyway. It's next door to Fiona's place.
- ◯ I didn't want to be the one to show you Janay's house, but you would've found it anyway. Its next door to Fiona's place.

UNIT ELEVEN

Crime doesn't pay

Focus

Direct and indirect speech; punctuating indirect speech

Grammar in use

In Canberra, ACT Policing recovered a 1.6-metre-tall fibreglass Utah raptor dinosaur which had been stolen last Thursday from Canberra's Gold Creek based National Dinosaur Museum. Museum manager Richard Mancuso is quoted by *The Canberra Times* as saying, **'We are exceptionally happy it has been found and it is great that the police will now be able to resolve the matter.' The thief said that he had stolen the dinosaur as part of a birthday prank and had planned to return it to the museum later that day.** He was said to be contrite and apologetic.

Adapted from http://en.wikinews.org/wiki/Stolen_Utahraptor_recovered_in_Australian_Capital_Territory

About grammar

Writers often have to give information about what people say or think. In order to do this they use **direct** or **indirect speech**.

- **Direct speech** is also known as **quoted speech** and is used when you say **exactly** what someone has said. The exact words that someone has spoken appear within quotation marks (' … '); *for example,* Richard Mancuso said, '**We are exceptionally happy it has been found and it is great that the police will now be able to resolve the matter.**' You looked at this in Unit 8.
- **Indirect speech** is also known as **reported speech**. Indirect speech **doesn't** use quotation marks to enclose what the person has said and doesn't have to be word for word (exact); *for example,* **The thief said that he had stolen the dinosaur as part of a birthday prank and had planned to return it to the museum later that day.** In indirect speech, **tense**, **word order** and **pronouns** may be different from those in the original spoken sentence, particularly if the direct speech is a **question**; for example, *The police asked, '***Are you** *sorry?'* → *The police asked if* **he was** *sorry*. In the newspaper text above, the thief would have actually said *'I* **stole** *the dinosaur … and* **planned** *to return it …'* . Sometimes you might need to leave out words or change words to make the sentence more elegant; for example, the sentence *He enquired 'Should you be here at all?'* would be better changed to *He asked if I should be there at all.*

Verb tense influences direct to indirect speech transitions.

- The **present tense** (*I travel*) usually changes to the **past simple** (*he travelled*) in reported speech; for example, *'I* **travel** *a lot in my job.'* → *He said that he* **travelled** *a lot in his job.*
- The **past tense** (*we lived*) usually changes to the **past perfect** (*they had lived*) in reported speech; for example, *'We* **lived** *in Canberra for five years.'* → *She told me they* **had lived** *in Canberra for five years.*
- The **present perfect tense** *(I have apologised)* also usually changes to the **past perfect** *(I had apologised)* in reported speech; for example, *'I* **have** *already* **apologised** *to the museum,' he said* → *He said that he* **had** *already* **apologised** *to the museum.*
- The **future tense** (*I will travel*) usually changes to the **conditional** (*I would travel*) in reported speech; for example, *'I* **will** *travel when I'm older' she said* → *She said that she* **would** *travel when she's older.*

Boost your grammar skills

1 Insert the correct verb in these examples of **i direct speech** (present tense) and **ii indirect speech** (past tense).

For example: i 'I ___am___ going to the museum,' she said.

ii She said she ___was___ going to the museum.

- **a** i The manager replied, 'We ________ not putting up with these conditions any longer.'
  - ii The manager said they ________ not going to put up with the conditions any longer.
- **b** i 'The dinosaur ________ very large,' said the thief. 'I hope it will fit in the truck'.
  - ii The thief said the dinosaur ________ very large. He hoped it ________ fit in the truck.
- **c** i 'I want you to return it now,' said John.
  - ii John said that he ________ you to return it now.
- **d** i 'Why do you need to take it?' inquired Lisa
  - ii Lisa wondered why he ________ ________ ________ it.

2 Circle the correct **indirect** speech version of these **direct** speech examples.

- **a** The manager said, 'The dinosaur belongs in the museum.'
  - i The manager said that the dinosaur had belonged in the museum.
  - ii The manager said that the dinosaur belonged in the museum.
- **b** 'We have seen a surprising amount of this sort of thing,' said the police officer.
  - i The police officer said that they had seen a surprising amount of this sort of thing.
  - ii The police officer said that they saw a surprising amount of this sort of thing.
- **c** Richard Mancuso said, 'I work at the museum.'
  - i Richard Mancuso said that he worked at the museum.
  - ii Richard Mancuso said that he works at the museum.
- **d** The police officer said, 'I have arrested a lot of people in my line of work.'
  - i The police officer said that she arrested a lot of people in her line of work.
  - ii The police officer said that she had arrested a lot of people in her line of work.
- **e** The thief said, 'I'm really sorry about all of this.'
  - i The thief said that he was really sorry about all of this.
  - ii The thief said that he is really sorry about all of this.
- **f** The museum manager said, 'We will be improving security at the museum.'
  - i The museum manager said that they will be improving security at the museum.
  - ii The museum manager said that they would be improving security at the museum.

3 Change the following examples of **direct** speech into **indirect** speech. Remember: you will need to adjust punctuation and possibly tense, word order and pronouns.

- **a** The reporter asked, 'How will the museum protect exhibits in the future?'

  ____

- **b** 'I have regretted this since it occurred', moaned the thief.

  ____

c The police officer said, 'We are extremely pleased to have located the dinosaur.'

____

d The thief admitted, 'I have been thinking of doing something like this for a while.'

____

e The museum manager exclaimed, 'We have never had anything like this happen before!'

____

4 Change the following examples of **indirect** speech into **direct** speech. Remember: you will need to adjust punctuation and possibly tense, word order and pronouns.

a Police said that they had recovered a 1.6-metre-tall dinosaur that had been stolen.

____

b The manager wondered what had happened to the dinosaur during its absence.

____

c The manager said he was exceptionally happy now.

____

d Dinosaur museum members said that they were relieved the dinosaur was back in its rightful place.

____

e The police asked the thief if he had stolen anything else.

____

5 Circlee the correct **indirect** speech for these direct speech **questions**.

a I said to him, 'Why don't you work hard?'

- **i** I asked him why didn't you work hard.
- **ii** I asked him why he didn't work hard.

b He enquired, 'When do you intend to return the dinosaur?'

- **i** He asked when I intended to return the dinosaur.
- **ii** He enquired, 'When do you intend to return the dinosaur?'

c 'Have you anything to tell me, young man?' asked the officer.

- **i** The officer asked the young man has he anything to tell him.
- **ii** The officer asked the young man if he had anything to tell him.

d 'Have you anything to say on behalf of the accused?' asked the judge.

- **i** The judge asked whether he has anything to say on behalf of the accused.
- **ii** The judge asked whether he had anything to say on behalf of the accused.

e The thief said to the police, 'What have I done to deserve so severe a punishment?'

- **i** The thief asked the police what he had done to deserve so severe a punishment.
- **ii** The thief asked the police what he did to deserve so severe a punishment.

Punctuation in use

When **Mark 'Banana' Smith**, a 16-year-old from the US, entered an internet cafe and demanded money, he claimed he had a gun hidden under his shirt.

The 'gun' was actually a banana. The café's owner, along with a customer, restrained Mark and called the police.

Mark anticipated **the police would shout, 'Put the gun down!'** so he ate the banana while he waited for them to arrive. **The police joked about charging the kid with 'destroying evidence'.** They also sang **Harry Belafonte's 'Banana Boat Song'** to him as they led him away.

About punctuation

- You looked at punctuating **direct speech** in Unit 8. Remember: direct speech is the exact words spoken by someone. Direct speech and its ending punctuation are all enclosed in quotation marks; for example, **'Put the gun down!'**
- **Indirect speech** does not need quotation marks. In general, **exclamation marks** and **question marks** will change to full stops when direct speech is changed into indirect speech; for example, **the police would shout, 'Put the gun down!'** becomes *the police would shout at him to put the gun down.*
- Quotation marks are not only used to mark the words people say. **Single quotation marks** or **italics** are used for the following special circumstances:
  - a **nickname** after someone's real name; for example, **Mark 'Banana' Smith**
  - an **unusual** or **particular** usage of a word or phrase; for example, **The 'gun' was actually a banana** and **The police joked about charging the kid with 'destroying evidence'**.
  - the **titles** of poems, songs, short stories and articles; for example, **Harry Belafonte's 'Banana Boat Song'**.
- Sometimes we need to use single quotation marks for the above reasons inside direct speech. You then must use double quotation marks instead. When the word or phrase enclosed in quotation marks occurs at the **end** of direct speech, you must remember to use the final quotation marks for the direct speech as well. Look at this example: *The café owner said, 'I'm just grateful that the gun wasn't real, although I could have lived without hearing "The Banana Boat Song!"'*

Boost your punctuation skills

1 Revise your knowledge of **direct speech** by correctly punctuating these sentences.

a Robbery is the crime of taking or attempting to take something of value by force or threat of force or by causing the victim to be fearful declared the police officer.

b The lawyer explained Robbery is different from other forms of theft such as burglary, shoplifting or car theft as it is violent in nature.

c Picking a victim's pocket is generally not considered robbery said Thomas because there is no use of fear and because robbery requires more force than that necessary simply to remove the property.

d Wikipedia states The most common situation is the hold-up, in which the robber threatens to shoot if valuables are not turned over.

e Robbery was one of the first crimes under English law to be made punishable by the government rather than through compensation explained the historian.

2 Add the missing **single quotation marks** to the following sentences.

a The word rob evolved through French from Late Latin words of Germanic origin.

b Highway robbery (or mugging) takes place outside or in a public place such as a footpath, street or car park.

c Criminal slang for robbery includes blagging, stick-up and steaming, the latter being organised robbery on underground train systems.

d Robberies have been depicted, sometimes graphically, in various forms of media, and several robbers have become pop icons, such as George Baby Face Nelson.

e The Highwayman by Alfred Noyes is a popular poem about an 18th-century robber.

3 Circle the correctly punctuated **sentence**.

a **i** 'Ben Hall was an Australian bushranger of the 19th century. He was known as "Brave Ben Hall" and has become part of Australian folklore,' explained the tour guide.

ii 'Ben Hall was an Australian bushranger of the 19th century. He was known as Brave Ben Hall and has become part of Australian folklore' explained the tour guide.

b **i** The teacher informed us that 'Hall's gang was joined by The Old Man (James Mount) and Dunleavy, neither of whom lasted long.'

ii The teacher informed us that Hall's gang was joined by 'The Old Man' (James Mount) and Dunleavy, neither of whom lasted long.

c **i** There is a cave in an isolated section of the Wedding Range, near Grenfell, 'that is known as Ben Hall's Cave,' he read aloud.

ii 'There is a cave in an isolated section of the Wedding Range, near Grenfell, that is known as Ben Hall's Cave,' he read aloud.

d **i** The historian told us that 'the most notable poem about Hall's life is 'Streets of Forbes', which has been recorded by numerous singers and groups. She also said that 'Others include 'The Ballad of Ben Hall's Gang, The Death of Ben Hall and The Ghost of Ben Hall."

ii The historian told us that the most notable poem about Hall's life is 'Streets of Forbes', which has been recorded by numerous singers and groups. She also said that others include 'The Ballad of Ben Hall's Gang', 'The Death of Ben Hall' and 'The Ghost of Ben Hall'.

4 Tick (✔) the correctly punctuated **sentences** and cross (✘) the incorrect sentences.

a The author said, 'My interest in bushrangers led me to research and write "The Betrayal and Death of Ben Hall".' ______

b The Bathurst Times said of the gang, Every new success is a source of pleasure to them and they are stimulated to the novelty of actions by desire to make history. ______

c The teacher explained that the exploits, capture and death of 'Brave' Ben Hall in the 1860s were part of Australian folklore. ______

d Reports from the time 'stated that there were plenty of sympathisers who 'offered' them safe hiding places and who in turn were often rewarded with a share of the goods.' ______

e 'Ben Hall was also seen as a "Robin Hood" figure, stealing from the rich and redistributing the booty to his supporters, family and friends,' read the student to the class. ______

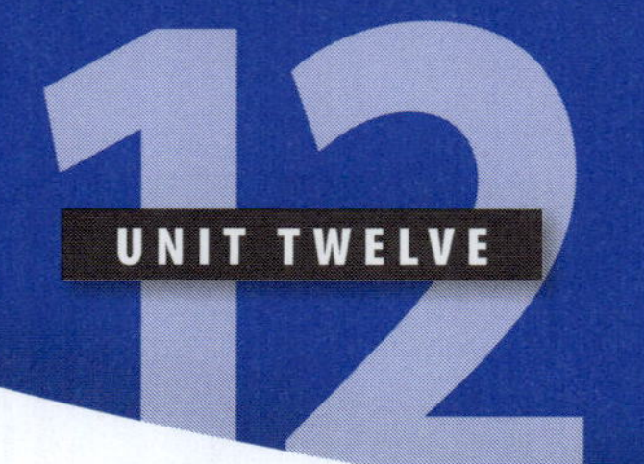

UNIT TWELVE

Review of *The Sapphires*

Focus

Modality; apostrophes of contraction

Grammar in use

The Sapphires is definitely the feel-good film of the year. It tells an Australian tale inspired by the real-life achievements of an Aboriginal girl-group of the 1960s that **will undoubtedly** make an impact beyond our shores. It is just **possible** that *The Sapphires* will beat box office records for the year.

Director Wayne Blair creates in *The Sapphires* a strong, offbeat sense of humour that truthfully reveals the rebellious spirit of the women and the music they sing. **To some extent**, any shortcomings are forgiven whenever the **always** enjoyable Jessica Mauboy gets near a microphone and the film's winning selection of original soul standards is heard.

The **likelihood** is high that *The Sapphires* will take out this year's Aussie films top spot—I **really** think you **ought** to make time to see it.

About grammar

- Words like *really, will, would, probably, certainly, unlikely, definitely, maybe, I guess* and *could* allow us to express how certain we are about what we are saying and how strongly we feel about it. This aspect of language is called **modality**.
- We use modality every day when we talk to each other; for example, *I'm definitely going; I might be going; I should go.* We also use it to express and modify **argument** and **opinion** in **academic** texts, such as essays and reports, and other **persuasive** texts, such as reviews, speeches and letters to the editor.
- The term **high modality** refers to the use of strong words such as *must, definitely* and *never* to express a **high** degree of certainty or strength of feeling; for example, *The film* **always** *impresses; The songs* **will never** *be forgotten.* High modality allows us to be more persuasive, but it needs to be used with care. If you use high modality too much in your writing, it may weaken your argument.
- The term **low modality** refers to the use of words such as *might* and *perhaps* to express a **low** degree of certainty or strength of feeling; for example, *The film* **may** *inspire others; It* **appears unlikely** *that the film will do well.* A **low modality** statement of opinion allows us to express our ideas with more **caution** and **reservation**.
- **Modality** appears in language as:
  - » **modal verbs** such as *could, might, may, have to, must, ought to, should, can, need to, shall, will* and *would*; for example, *It tells an Australian tale … that* **will** *undoubtedly make an impact beyond our shores; I really think you* **ought** *to make time to see it.*
  - » **nouns** such as *likelihood, possibility, probability* and *certainty*; for example, *The* **likelihood** *is high that* The Sapphires *will take out this year's Aussie films top spot.*
  - » **adjectives** such as *possible, probable, definite, sure, certain* and *likely*; for example, *It is just* **possible** *that* The Sapphires *will beat box office records for the year.*

» **adverbs** such as *possibly, really, definitely, surely, perhaps, sometimes, seldom, often, always* and *never*; for example, *It tells an Australian tale … that will* **undoubtedly** *make an impact beyond our shores; I* **really** *think you ought to make time to see it.*

» **phrases** such as *I guess, I suppose, I think* and *to some extent*; for example, **To some extent**, *any shortcomings are forgiven.*

✸ It is important to choose these words and phrases carefully when writing. It is often the careful **combination** of verbs, adverbs and adjectives that heighten and strengthen, or weaken and reduce, the potency of an idea; for example, **I believe it will undoubtedly** *make an impact beyond our shores;* **It is quite probable that it will** *make an impact beyond our shores;* **I guess it could** *make an impact beyond our shores.*

Boost your grammar skills

1 Place the following list of **modal verbs** and **adverbs** into the table.

sometimes ought to will cannot would might possibly absolutely must always never maybe often could perhaps should is

Low degree of certainty	Moderate/medium degree of certainty	High degree of certainty
might	should	is

2 Underline any **modal words or expressions** you find in the following sentences.

a This multi-talented artist could possibly be one of Australia's hottest young creative exports.

b The album is extremely personal and I've definitely worked hard on it all year.

c The certainty is that I have really pushed myself—I could have failed but I always try my best.

d It ought to be a difficult journey, even for those with immense talent.

e I should be afraid of the possibility of failure, but I will never give up.

3 Use one of the following **modal verbs** in each of the following sentences. The bracketed information will help you choose.

should might should couldn't can't might must

For example: Film prices ___will___ increase next year. (are going to)

a The reviewer ________________ finish her analysis because she had not viewed the whole film. (found it impossible)

b The reviewer ________________ have a positive attitude. (There is low possibility.)

c Locally made films ________________ be seen at international festivals. (It is suggested.)

d He ________________ be the person they saw! (It is surely not possible.)

e It has been open for four months, so the film ________________ be very popular. (It is highly probable.)

f He ________________ see the film over the weekend. (There is some possibility.)

g The film is by far the best one of the year so a trophy ________________ be awarded. (It is recommended.)

4 Match the following sentences to their correct responses.

a The film got a great response.

b The girls are finally on their way to Vietnam.

c Fiona's seen the film so talk to her.

d He watches movies all night you know.

e I was thinking about what Kai said about the film.

f I can't see the film listed on the noticeboard.

They must be very excited.

That can't be healthy.

He may be right.

The director must be thrilled.

She should be able to tell you about it.

It may have been cancelled.

5 Write *H* for high or *L* for low to describe the **modality** level of the following sentences.

a *The Sapphires* is an example of the type of film this country really should be making more of. ______

b The music is definitely charming and the music so inspiring that you have to cut it a break. ______

c Dave thinks the girls might be soul singers and that their big break could come from performing for the troops in Vietnam. ______

d *The Sapphires* will have you laughing, crying and celebrating the achievement of these four amazing Aboriginal women. ______

e I suppose of all the actors in *The Sapphires*, Mauboy could fare the best. ______

6 Put these sentences in order from the strongest, most certain expression of feeling (1) to the weakest, least certain (5).

a The films shown at the festival often showcase the talent of local Australian actors. ______

b The films shown at the festival rarely showcase the talent of local Australian actors. ______

c The films shown at the festival sometimes showcase the talent of local Australian actors. ______

d The films shown at the festival always showcase the talent of local Australian actors. ______

7 Change the following sentences from **high modality** to **low modality** (in other words, make them less certain). There is more than one way to do this.

a In the film, the girls never let insensitive comments get them down.

____

b The original play has become a movie that will be irresistible.

____

c Without a doubt, actor Chris O'Dowd has reached an emotional peak in this role.

____

d The songs are absolutely charming and enjoyable.

____

e You will definitely enjoy both the music and the performances.

____

Punctuation in use

In an interview with *The Sydney Morning Herald*, Jessica Mauboy talked of discovering her Indigenous heritage: 'We never really got to know our clan. **We're** just finding our family tree now,' she is reported as saying. Interestingly, she said that *The Sapphires* inspired her to explore her **mum's** culture. 'Emotionally, I had to do it because I **didn't** really know, well, me, yet.'

Mauboy told the interviewer that she takes her responsibilities seriously and that **there's** an Indigenous community that she visits to sing to. **'It's** amazing to see them opening up and actually having a voice,' she said. 'I feel like there is a generation that's starting to feel, no matter what colour we are, we can do it. All those kids, **they're** driven. They just want to chase it.'

Adapted from
http://www.smh.com.au/entertainment/movies/finding-her-true-voice-20120804-23loz.html

About punctuation

- **Apostrophes of contraction** are used to show that letters are missing in words; for example, *wasn't, he's, can't,* **it's** and *I'm*. We **shorten or contract** some words for ease of communication by leaving out or **omitting** letters; for example, **We're** *(We are) just finding our family tree now.*
- **Contractions** often occur with **pronouns** (and ***here/there***) and **auxiliary** (helping) verbs; for example, *I have → I've, we are → we're, they had → they'd, there is → there's, I will → I'll, he would → he'd;* for example, **there's** *an Indigenous community that she visits to sing to.*
- Note that ***'s*** can mean *is* or *has*; for example, *It's interesting.* (It is interesting.) *It's been interesting.* (It has been interesting.)
- The contraction ***'d*** can mean *had* or *would*; for example, *She'd always loved singing.* (She had always loved singing.) *She'd love to perform overseas.* (She would love to perform overseas.)
- **Contractions** are also used to form **negative modal verbs** by adding *not* after an auxiliary verb, such as *is not → isn't, does not → doesn't*; for example, *I* **didn't** *really know.* Two irregular contractions are *will not → won't* and *cannot → can't.*
- Take care when writing contractions with the word **have**. When spoken they sound like the weak pronunciation of the preposition *of*, and they can be mistakenly written that way; for example, *could've → could have*, not 'could of', and *would've → would have*, not 'would of'.
- **Contractions** are also made when auxiliary verbs such as ***is*** and ***was*** appear after a **noun**; for example, *Jessica's here.* (Jessica is here.) Take care not to confuse **apostrophes of possession** with **apostrophes of contraction** as they have quite different purposes. (You learnt about apostrophes of possession in Unit 7.) Always think about what the apostrophe means. For example:
  The Sapphires inspired me to explore my **mum's** *culture.* (apostrophe of possession)
  My **mum's** *very special to me.* (apostrophe of contraction)
- Beware of confusion between:
  - ***it's*** (*it is/it has*) and ***its*** (possessive pronoun meaning 'belonging to it'). If you can't replace *it's* with *it is* or *it has* in the sentence, then you need *its*; for example, **It's** [it is] *time for* **its** *haircut as* **it's** [it has] *been too long.*
  - ***you're*** (*you are*) and ***your*** (possessive pronoun meaning 'belonging to you'). If you can't replace *you're* with *you are* in the sentence, then you need *your*; for example, **You're** [you are] *such a great singer and I would like to be* **your** friend.
  - ***they're*** (*they are*) and ***there*** (an adverb used when referring to a place) or ***their*** (possessive adjective); for example, **They're** *going to the concert in* **their** *car that's over* **there**.

Boost your punctuation skills

1 Write the full form of each **contraction** on the lines.

- **a** (We're) __________ __________ just finding our family tree now.
- **b** (It's) __________ __________ strange having all those people come up to you.
- **c** She (would've) __________ __________ done anything to find out.
- **d** She could be a stage performer, and (that's) __________ __________ possibly where (she's) __________ __________ meant to be.
- **e** I (won't) __________ __________ let other people drag me down and (I'll) __________ __________ always try my best.

2 Write the **contraction** of the words in brackets on the lines.

- **a** (What is) ______________ so amazing about Eurovision is that it allows you to take a bit of a risk.
- **b** It was a once-in-a-lifetime opportunity that (I will) ______________ never ever forget.
- **c** Mauboy nailed her chance to sing a song (she had) ______________ written just for the world's kitschiest music competition.
- **d** The interviewer said, '(Do not) ______________ you know (you are) ______________ not part of Europe?'
- **e** I (do not) ______________ know many Aussies who (cannot) ______________ laugh when they embarrass themselves.

3 Punctuate the following examples of **contractions** and **possession** correctly using the apostrophe.

- **a** I think Beyoncés fantastic and Im completely nowhere near where she is, but I aspire to be like her. I think shes amazing.
- **b** Mauboy couldve become the face of an alcohol brand but she believed it wouldve sent the wrong message to Indigenous communities.
- **c** Ive recently been home and spent some time with my dad. I miss that I cant see him more often and were definitely going back soon. Hed really love that.
- **d** It isnt too tricky—Ive grown up singing and when I sing Im proud. Its a great feeling.
- **e** It was the most fun weve ever had in the studio and we couldnt have achieved it without everyones support.

4 Correctly punctuate the following sentences using apostrophes of contraction and apostrophes of possession. After each sentence, write *C* if you have added an **apostrophe of contraction** and *P* if you have added an **apostrophe of possession**.

- **a** At the age of 14, Mauboys talents were exposed through the Telstra Road to Tamworth competition where shed impressed everyone. ______ ______
- **b** Mauboys now a member of the girl group Young Divas, replacing one of the groups original members. ______ ______
- **c** Mauboys made several visits to Yipirinya School since the announcement that shes their official ambassador. ______ ______

d Were pleased to announce that two dollars from every sale of Mauboys nail polish was donated to Childrens Hospital Foundations Australia. ______ ______

e Monday nights catch-up wasnt the first time Mauboy has come face to face with her idol. ______ ______

5 Write the contraction ***it's*** or the pronoun ***its*** in the gaps as necessary.

Have you heard the new album? __________ amazing. __________ been played on most radio stations around Australia and __________ bound to break domestic sales records. The album has such a cool look. __________ cover is filled with images and colours and __________ by far my favourite album of the year. __________ definitely on my list of recommendations and __________ unique sound will certainly be popular.

6 Write the contraction ***you're*** or the pronoun ***your*** in the gaps as necessary.

Hi Jessica! We are huge fans of __________ music and can't wait to see __________ concert later this year. We think __________ more than just a pop singer, and we really admire all the work __________ doing with Australian youth. __________ really turning into a fantastic actress as well! I've already ordered __________ new album and can't wait to listen to it.

7 Write the contraction ***they're***, the possessive adjective ***their*** or the adverb ***there*** in the gaps as necessary.

I just spoke to Casey and Tiana and ____________________ going to be at the concert too! I hope they bring ____________________ CDs to get signed. Have you been ____________________ before? It's my second time. The last time I nearly left my phone ____________________. I was frantic with worry, but the concert organisers used ____________________ security guards to help me locate it. I think ____________________ fantastic!

8 Place apostrophes of **contraction** where needed in the following text.

Ive always loved singing although I didnt always know I would be successful. Fames a difficult thing and Im always trying to just be myself but its hard. Theres always something new to do and Ive really enjoyed working with young Indigenous people. Theyll say Im a role model but for me its also about being creative. Its about the music and the fans. I hope theyll listen and enjoy the music and remember all the great things theyve got in their lives.

UNIT THIRTEEN

Communication and technology

Focus
Cohesive writing; colons and semicolons

Grammar in use

Communication is one of the most important factors shaping society's future. Our lives would be meaningless without it as communication influences our ability to live, thrive and survive. **It is through interaction that we understand** ourselves and others. **In addition, it is the vehicle that allows us** to remember past events, exist in the present, and that allows us to hope for the future.

Communication in modern society is dominated by technology. As a result, there is less value placed on respectful and quality **communication,** and time spent in meaningful social interaction has decreased dramatically, within the family, the workplace and the school environment.

About grammar

- **Cohesive writing** is writing that is **unified.** It is writing which **hangs together as a whole** and which makes reading easy, because the **ideas are clearly linked** from one sentence to the next and from one paragraph to the next. You can achieve cohesion in your writing by using the following language devices.
- **Transition signals** are words and phrases that guide the reader from one idea to another; for example, *in addition, furthermore, as a result, finally* and *nevertheless.* They are used to join **sentences**, **idea groups** and **paragraphs**, and to create logical relationships between ideas. For example:

  It is through interaction that we … **In addition**, *it is the vehicle that allows us …*
  Communication in modern society is dominated by technology. **As a result**, there is less value …
- Transition signals are used to:
  - » **add information**; for example, **in addition**, *moreover, furthermore, besides, in fact* and *also*
  - » **contrast ideas**; for example, *on the other hand, in contrast* and *nevertheless*
  - » **compare ideas**; for example, *similarly* and *also*
  - » **conclude ideas**; for example, *in conclusion, in summary* and *finally*
  - » **order by time**; for example, *after that, before that, then, at first, since, firstly, lastly* and *finally*
  - » **show the result** of something; for example, **as a result**, *consequently, therefore, thus* and *hence.*
- **Repetition of key words** is another useful device to achieve cohesion in a text. In the above text, the key word **communication** occurs four times in two short paragraphs; **society** occurs twice. This repetition establishes and helps us keep track of the two main themes of the text—communication and how it affects our lives. In the paragraph to follow we would expect to find the word **technology** occur again.

- **Reference via pronouns** helps the reader keep track of **nouns** introduced in a text. Pronouns such as *he, she, they, them, him, her, it, this, these* and *those* help writers **refer** back and forward to key nouns without always repeating them. You learnt about pronouns in Unit 2. In academic writing, these pronouns are crucial for linking ideas within and between sentences and from one paragraph to the next.

  In the following sentences the key noun **communication** is replaced by the reference pronoun **it**, and **society's** is replaced by the reference pronoun **our**:

  Communication *is one of the most important factors shaping* **society's** *future.* **Our** *lives would be meaningless without* **it**.

- Using **synonyms** for key nouns and verbs is another way to avoid too much repetition and monotony of expression. For example, in the following sentences the key noun **communication** is replaced by the synonym **interaction**:

  Our lives would be meaningless without it as **communication** *influences our ability …*
  It is through **interaction** *that we understand …*

Boost your grammar skills

1 Look at the following sentences. Underline the **transition signal**. Then, using the information above, write down the transition signal's purpose. The transition signal does not always occur at the beginning of a sentence.

- **a** Technology has become an integral part of all our lives. Consequently, attitudes towards 'old' ways of communicating are changing. ____________
- **b** We may never return to a time when the written word was so valued; however, we must always strive to maintain a high level of language and communication. ____________
- **c** Conversely, it is still necessary to learn about grammar and punctuation, as these are still considered important for effective communication. ____________
- **d** In conclusion, it's important to understand when to use social media language, and when it is unsuitable. ____________
- **e** In addition, student literacy rates may be falling because of the language of social media. ____________

2 From each pair of **transition signals** in parentheses, choose the one that combines each pair of sentences into a single sentence that makes sense.

- **a** How we speak is significant. What we say is also important. (as a result/furthermore)
- **b** It's great that technology connects us to family, friends and business. Make your first priority the people who you are present with. (nevertheless/after that)
- **c** Firstly, decide what words are suitable at that time. You should proceed with your communication. (consequently/then)
- **d** Most people agree that technology has made communication easier. You should still take the time to plan what you are going to say. (in addition/however)
- **e** Not everyone wants to hear your conversation. Be aware of where you are when using a mobile phone. (therefore/moreover)

3 Insert a **reference pronoun** as needed in the following sentences.

a Raul explained how ________________ changed his routine during one of his business phone calls. Instead of a conference call, ________________ decided to switch to video because ________________ allowed him to see his callers face to face.

b Patricia found that the ability to communicate with her work colleagues using social networking and to be able to text ________________ during conference calls and see ________________ on skype has enabled ________________ to feel connected.

c Social media is surprising in that ________________ fills a gap many workers feel when writing cold, impersonal emails as their primary source of communication.

d The promise of the virtual workplace fails some people. ________________ sometimes miss out on opportunities for ________________ to improve their work experience.

e Collaboration used to only occur between people in the same office. Today, ________________ occurs between multiple people all over the world at the same time.

4 Tick (✔) the sentences that use **reference pronouns** correctly and cross (✘) those that don't.

a A new generation of communication technology is here. They are introducing a new way to work that is influencing workplaces worldwide. ______

b Technology is also useful for completing work from home. Workers use it to complete tasks remotely and they save much time by avoiding commuting. ______

c A high percentage of people work from home using technology. What's interesting is that in most cases he is mostly using outdated technology. ______

d Technology has boosted efficiency in factories and homes. It has improved research and study opportunities and it has provided people with an abundance of knowledge. I believe we have greatly benefited from it. ______

e Technology is what makes learning so exciting. It has really widened productivity and possibility for students. They also make employment more interesting. ______

5 It's important that synonyms don't alter the essential message of a sentence. In the following sentences, circle the **synonym** that best represents the underlined key noun in the first sentence.

a People take technology for granted; however, it is also important to know the <u>appropriate</u> time to access it. You should remember that there are proper/accurate/perfect occasions when it is best placed aside.

b The <u>way</u> we communicate is still important. Just because the technique/method/procedure is now instant and fast does not mean that grammar and spelling should be disregarded.

c <u>Always</u> be aware of what you've written. At all times/constantly/repetitively double-check your ideas before you hit 'send.'

d If you don't want anyone to hear your <u>conversation</u>, chances are they don't want to listen to your discussion/debate/dispute either.

e Sometimes an email is <u>suitable</u> for sending information; sometimes a written letter is more suitable. It is essential to consider what is the most satisfactory/appropriate/pleasing method for the occasion.

6 In the following sentences, write on the line a suitable **synonym** for the underlined key **noun**. You may need to use a thesaurus.

For example: Conversation doesn't occur face to face as often as people would like. Instead, exchanges often occur by emails and texts and this can make it difficult to really get to know people.

a There are many who complain about the way technology creates pressure in everyday lives. The challenge is to find ways to reduce the ________________ so that people can create a work and life balance.

b The answer is not to remove technology altogether, but to ________________ technology that inhibits natural human behaviour.

c One of the main predictors of employee happiness is whether they have close relationships at work. This shows that real ________________, compared to those on social media, are still important to people.

d Technology is particularly useful for locating information instantly. People have immediate access to the ________________ they need, be it for business, study or social purposes.

7 The following sentences form part of a paragraph, but they are out of order. Number them from 1 to 5 in the order they should appear within the paragraph. Underline the words and phrases that helped you sequence the information.

_____ All of these things are mostly positive and give you further opportunities for connecting with your friends.

_____ In conclusion, it is better to use a nickname as this is safer than providing your real name and it also makes it harder for people to identify you

_____ Communication technologies such as mobile phones, email, blogs and social networking websites most likely play an important part in your social life.

_____ However, communication technologies can contribute towards unwanted attention and even unpleasantness.

_____ For example, once you put images or comments on a website or send them in an email, you have no further control over that material or how widely it is distributed.

Punctuation in use

The ways in which we communicate have changed in the past few decades thanks to technology. **Just think about how much you use the following: texting, the internet and social media.** These have changed the way we work, the way we live, and the way we make and maintain friendships. **The words 'information' and 'communication' are often used interchangeably but they actually mean quite different things: information is something given out while communication is something shared.**

For some people, technology is a cause for anxiety; they are fearful about the future of human interaction. They are concerned, for example, that people appear to be more interested in events and friends thousands of kilometres away than in what's going on in their immediate world. **They see that technology can influence individuals to withdraw from the physical world; furthermore, they fear it can promote antisocial behaviour and weaken real relationships. Albert Einstein understood the danger to our society of technology. He said: 'It has become appallingly obvious that our technology has exceeded our humanity.'**

About punctuation

Two useful types of punctuation, especially in formal writing, are the **colon** and the **semicolon**. Although these look similar and have similar names, their functions are completely different.

A **colon** consists of two dots (**:**), one above the other.

* A **colon** is often used to introduce a **list** of items; for example, **Just think about how much you use the following: texting, the internet and social media.**
* A **colon** may also be used between independent clauses when the second sentence **paraphrases** or **expands** on the first sentence; for example, **The words 'information' and 'communication' are often used interchangeably but they actually mean quite different things: information is something given out while communication is something shared.**
* A colon can also be used to set up a long **quotation** (more than about six words); for example, **Albert Einstein understood the danger to our society of technology. He said: 'It has become appallingly obvious that our technology has exceeded our humanity.'**

A **semicolon** consists of a comma with a dot above it (**;**). A semicolon can always be replaced by a full stop.

* The semicolon is often used to join **two independent clauses** containing closely related ideas, and often replaces *and* or *but*; for example, **For some people, technology is a cause for anxiety;** [and] **they are fearful about the future of human interaction.** When we use a semicolon in this way, it is often because we want to make the reader think about the **relationship** between the two clauses.
* Using semicolons to join sentences in this way also helps to **maintain the theme** of a sentence, avoid **abrupt**, short sentences, and avoid **overuse** of *and* or *but*.
* One more very common use of the semicolon is to **join two clauses** using a **transition signal** such as *in addition, otherwise, however, therefore,* or *on the other hand*; for example, **They see that technology can influence individuals to withdrawal from the physical world; furthermore, they fear it can promote antisocial behaviour and weaken real relationships.**

Boost your punctuation skills

1 Insert a **colon** where necessary in the following sentences.

a Technology has contributed to changes in our lives we now talk less, stay indoors more and spend time creating online personas.

b The parent's intentions were clear no one would be using their devices during dinner.

c My teacher demanded 'Why are you using your phone during my lesson?'

d Tamika created her invitation online. Only four classmates were invited Lisa, Rolf, Hasheem and Maia.

e Albert Einstein also said 'The human spirit must prevail over technology.'

2 Insert a **semicolon** where necessary in the following sentences.

- **a** Plenty of students had contributed online to the class blog Alyssa wanted to be one of them.
- **b** The most significant impact of technology on communication is the internet for example, it allows us to send emails and chat.
- **c** Technology is amazing however, it has contributed to loneliness for some who feel isolated.
- **d** Technology is no longer only a tool for survival it has turned into a source of communication and entertainment.
- **e** Younger generations are participating in a massive, unintentional social experiment the long-term effects of this are largely unknown.

3 In each of the following sentences insert either a **colon** or a **semicolon**.

- **a** Computers and the internet have eased the process of creating and editing documents. Think how often you use these tools spell check, grammar check, cut and paste, and word count.
- **b** The internet has increased the speed of communication consequently, the costs are reduced drastically.
- **c** The small keyboards on mobile phones make typing difficult and have resulted in a radical shortening of words there is now little or no observance of traditional grammatical rules.
- **d** Communication has become concise and short communication is now something achieved quickly and instantly.
- **e** Technology has brought down the costs of communication significantly as a result, it has improved people's access.

4 Tick (✔) the following sentences that use **colons** and **semicolons** correctly and cross (✘) those that don't.

- **a** People are now able to communicate instantly; and they are more likely to use their smart phone when doing so. ______
- **b** Ancient people used images as early written communication: these writings were usually; on stone. ______
- **c** In the pre-information technology days; a document often required re-typing on the typewriter before the final version. ______
- **d** Sending a letter to someone who lived elsewhere required a visit to the post office and a postage stamp; faster methods such as telegrams were expensive and you couldn't write much. ______
- **e** Bill Watterson said: 'All this modern technology just makes people try to do everything at once.' ______

5 Insert **colons** and **semicolons** where necessary in the following short paragraph.

> There is increasing interest in how mobile phone use in schools influences student achievement as a result, some school communities are calling for a complete ban of phones. This is an ongoing debate across the world some schools are showing concern for the use of phones, while others are more certain the use of phones is of educational benefit. A representative from the Department of Education has stated 'Phones should be discouraged unless they can be integrated into the learning program.' Some benefits of banning mobile phones in schools have been found to include the following improved student achievement higher concentration levels and happier, more engaged students.

UNIT FOURTEEN

Shakespeare's theatre

Focus

Clarity or ambiguity of expression; abbreviations and acronyms

Grammar in use

Note: this text includes sentence errors.

The works of William Shakespeare are considered to be some of the finest literature ever written. **Writing more than 400 years ago, his 37 plays covered tragedy, comedy and history.** These plays established a foundation for many works of literature for centuries to come. Shakespeare also **wrote down** over 150 poems (called sonnets). Amongst other things, Shakespeare's work has given us a glimpse into **past history** with his plays about the kings of England and about ancient lands and times.

During his lifetime, **Shakespeare enjoyed writing, acting and was involved in theatre productions. We know less about the personal life of Shakespeare than other famous writers.** However, his writing we do know. Today, Shakespeare **still remains** the person most people consider to be the best writer in the English language.

About grammar

Whenever you write it is important to express yourself with **clarity**, but it is especially important when writing academic and formal texts. Writing with clarity means writing in a concise, intelligent and direct way, so that it is easy for your reader to follow your meaning. Below are four common writing errors that you should avoid to ensure you are being **clear** in your academic writing.

- **Ambiguity** arises from using a word, phrase or sentence with more than one meaning. Ambiguity confuses your reader. For example, **We know less about the personal life of Shakespeare than other famous writers** is ambiguous. It is unclear whether we know less about the personal life of Shakespeare than other writers know about him, or we know less about the personal life of Shakespeare than we do about the personal life of other famous writers. The sentence becomes clearer when it is restructured: *We know less about the personal life of Shakespeare than about the personal lives of other famous writers.*
- **Dangling modifiers** are a particular kind of ambiguity. **Modifiers** are words and phrases which give additional detail about nouns and pronouns in a sentence (typically the subjects and objects). In clear, logical sentences you usually find modifiers close to the target words they are intended to describe. For example, *Looking into the past,* **we** *find a rich source of information* and *Performing the same play night after night,* **he** *quickly tired of his role.*

  The term *dangling modifier* refers to a group of words (typically at the start of the sentence) which does not refer logically to the noun or pronoun that is closest to it or, in some cases, to any target word at all. The modifier 'dangles' because the missing or incorrect target word leaves nothing for the modifier to describe; for example: **Writing more than 400 years ago,** *his 37 plays covered tragedy, comedy and history.* The introductory group of words *Writing more than 400 years ago* do not logically link to the target words *his 37 plays.*

Fixing a dangling modifier may require adding something new so that the modifier has a target word to describe; for example, Writing more than 400 years ago, **Shakespeare created** *37 plays* **that** *covered tragedy, comedy and history.*

Other examples of dangling modifiers and their possible corrections are:

Walking to the theatre, the cafes looked charming. (As I was walking to the theatre, I saw some charming cafes.)

Reaching the end of the performance, the crowd applauded. (When the performance ended, the crowd applauded.)

Not knowing his lines, the audience walked out. (The audience walked out when they realised the actor did not know his lines.)

- **Redundancy** occurs when particular words added to a text do not add anything to its meaning or content. Redundancy is the use of language that can be **removed** without loss of meaning.
  For example:

  Shakespeare also **wrote down**—*wrote* is adequate, *down* is unnecessary
  ...glimpse into **past history**—*history* is adequate, *past* is unnecessary
  Shakespeare **still remains** *the person—remains* is adequate, *still* is unnecessary.

  These **extra words** have the effect of making ideas unnecessarily wordy and indirect. Other commonly used examples include: *thoughts and ideas*; *advance planning*; *actual fact*; *basic essentials*; *difficult dilemma*; *rough estimate*; *repeat again*; *unintended mistake.*

- **Parallel structure** is the repetition of a particular grammatical arrangement within a sentence; for example, *Shakespeare enjoyed* **writing**, **acting** *and* **involving** *himself in theatre productions* (parallel *ing* words).

  In the text above, a **non-parallel** structure is used: *Shakespeare enjoyed* **writing**, **acting** *and* **was involved** *in theatre productions.* Maintaining parallel structure adds power and clarity to your writing as these **regular word patterns** increase the readability of your ideas.

  Another example is:

  The students liked to watch the rehearsals, listen to the actors' discussions, and then watching the final performance. (non-parallel)

  The students liked to watch the rehearsals, listen to the actors' discussions, and then watch the final performance. (parallel)

Boost your grammar skills

1 One sentence in each pair is completely **clear** (**unambiguous**). Tick (✔) that sentence.

a **i** When Lia and Cate arrived at the theatre, she told her she didn't have a ticket. ______
ii When Lia and Cate arrived at the theatre, Lia told her she didn't have a ticket. ______

b **i** He loves the dog more than his wife does. ______
ii He loves the dog more than his wife. ______

c **i** I saw a man on the TV with my glasses. ______
ii I used my glasses to see a man on the TV. ______

d **i** Look at the cat that has one eye. ______
ii Look at the cat with one eye. ______

e **i** The teacher said on Monday there would be a test. ______
ii The teacher said that next Monday there would be a test. ______

2 Rewrite each of the following so there is only **one possible meaning**. You may need to add or change words.

For example: I saw a man on the hill with binoculars.
I saw a man on the hill wearing binoculars.

a The lamb is ready to eat.

____

b Visiting neighbours can be boring.

____

c Thief gets 12 months in guitar case.

____

d An old car enthusiast visited the antiques showroom.

____

e This is my mother's photograph.

____

3 Tick (✔) the sentences below which contain **dangling modifiers**. Cross (✘) those that don't.

a Studying for the test tomorrow, the time was running out. ______

b Searching my room, my copy of the play was found. ______

c Reaching the end of the play, we were then allowed to watch the film. ______

d Thinking about Shakespeare's effect, we decided we had learnt a lot from reading his plays. ______

e Reading through the story, the play was very long. ______

4 Rewrite the following sentences that contain **dangling modifiers** to make their meaning clearer. There is more than one way to do this.

a Laughing hysterically, the play was very funny.

____

b Crossing the stage, the costume fell down around the actor's ankles.

____

c While standing in line, thunder boomed loudly.

____

d After singing on stage, the audience applauded the performance.

____

e Totally destroyed by the fire, he had to rebuild the theatre.

____

5 Tick (✔) the sentence in each pair below that contains **no redundant language**.

a **i** He carefully examined each and every word. ______
ii He carefully examined each word to make sure there were no errors. ______

b **i** During the last performance, the lead actor deviated from her routine. ______
ii During the last performance, the actor deviated from her regular routine. ______

c **i** The play set for study that term specifically targeted ideas about multiculturalism. ______
ii The teachers agreed that a play set for study that term would target ideas about multiculturalism. ______

d **i** After 1530 the play was not staged again for more than 200 years. ______

ii Despite its popularity, the play was not staged for more than 200 years. ______

e **i** The play's audience had increased up by 30% over the last three weeks. ______

ii The play's audience had increased by 30% over the last three weeks. ______

6 Underline the **redundant words** in the following sentences.

a I'm absolutely certain the students decided to return again for a second time to the theatre.

b Thanks to their joint collaboration, the university found the handwritten manuscript in the destroyed ruins of the writer's house, which was a great end result.

c As an added bonus, the jokes were designed to hit their intended targets with precise precision.

d They possibly might pack a lunch and bring along their own blanket for the outdoor performance.

e The presence of the King at the performance was an unexpected surprise as he still remains popular.

7 Tick (✔) the sentences below that use a **parallel structure**. Rewrite the incorrect sentences to form parallel structures.

a The audience not only like to be amused, but they also like to see tenderness. ______

b The actor was asked to prepare quickly, thoroughly and be very accurate. ______

c Shakespeare included characters who liked to fight, to eat and who enjoyed dancing. ______

d The teacher said that he was a good reader because he paused at the right moments, used his voice with expression, and is always looking up at the class. ______

e The director told the actors that they should get a lot of sleep, that they should learn their lines, and to try to relax before the show. ______

Punctuation in use

The Australian Elizabethan Theatre Trust (**AETT**) was set up in September 1954 under the guidance of the General Manager of the Australian Broadcasting Commission (**ABC**) and the Editor of *The Sydney Morning Herald* (**SMH**). It aimed to create an administration for drama, opera and ballet companies nationally.

The Trust played a key role in establishing high culture in Australia through its involvement in setting up what is now known as Opera Australia in 1956 and, with JC Williamson **Ltd,** the Australian Ballet School (**ABS**).

Adapted from https://en.wikipedia.org/wiki/Australian_Elizabethan_Theatre_Trust

About punctuation

- An **abbreviation** is a **shortened form** of a word or words. Abbreviations can be made from:
  - the **first letters of the original words**; for example, **AETT** (The Australian Elizabethan Theatre Trust) , **ABC** (Australian Broadcasting Commission), **SMH** (*Sydney Morning Herald*).
  - the **first few letters**; for example, *admin.* (administration), *cont.* (continued).
  - from **selected letters**; for example, **Ltd** (limited), *c/o* (*care of*), *dcd* (deceased).

- Some abbreviations are made into **words** called **acronyms**. Acronyms are words made up of the first letters of the originating term or title's **main words** without any full stops; for example, **IMAX** (*Image Maximum*), **radar** (*RAdio Detecting And Ranging*), **Qantas** (*Queensland and Northern Territory Aerial Services*), **scuba** (*Self-Contained Underwater Breathing Apparatus*).
- **Abbreviations** can be used for **note-taking** during study so that you do not need to write everything word for word. You can abbreviate by **leaving out most articles and conjunctions** (*the, a, and, an, but*) and **using abbreviations** for commonly used words and phrases; for example, *ach't* (achievement), *bk* (book), *c* or *cent.* (century), *concl.* (conclusion) and *diffic.* (difficult).
- An **abbreviation is followed by a full stop** if the last letter is **not** the last letter of the original word; for example, *dep.* (departure), *disc.* (discount).
- An **abbreviation has no full stop** if the last letter of the original and of the abbreviation are the same; for example, *hdqrs* (headquarters), *hwy* (highway).
- **Abbreviations** are sometimes used to **shorten common phrases**, but often the original words are Latin. So the abbreviation of *for example* is *e.g.*, which stands for *exempli gratia*. Other such abbreviations are *i.e.* (*id est* meaning 'that is'), *etc.* (*et cetera* meaning 'and so on'), *am* (*ante meridian* meaning 'before noon'), *pm* (*post meridian* meaning 'after noon').
- Abbreviations can be used in both **formal** and **informal** writing but the context determines whether or not an abbreviation is appropriate. New forms of abbreviation have come about in recent years, such as for the purpose of texting on mobile phones. **Texting language** contains many abbreviations and these new forms have found their way into some other informal kinds of written communication. Examples are *atm* (at the moment), *b4* (before), *brb* (be right back), *btw* (by the way). It is important to remember that text language is **not acceptable** in formal writing such as essays, exams and reports.

Boost your punctuation skills

1 Write the commonly used **abbreviations** for the following:

a in charge ____________ **b** Incorporated ____________
c Junior ____________ **d** kilojoule ____________
e kilometres per hour ____________ **f** accommodation ____________
g December ____________ **h** association ____________
I Doctor ____________ **j** Professor ____________
k milligram ____________

2 Write the meaning of the following mathematical, scientific and general **abbreviations** and **symbols**.

a $\neq$ ____________ **b** $\therefore$ ____________
c $\because$ ____________ **d** < ____________
e °C ____________ **f** ~ ____________
g dB ____________ **h** ft ____________
i @ ____________ **j** w/o ____________
k 8 ____________

3 What do these **abbreviations** mean?

a UN ______________________ b VIP ______________________

c ET ______________________ d FAQ ______________________

e RAM ______________________ f LCD ______________________

g ID ______________________ h WHO ______________________

i DOB ______________________ j AEDST ______________________

k SBS ______________________ l MC ______________________

m MP ______________________ n GM ______________________

4 **Rewrite** the following information using **abbreviations** appropriately. You may include some of your own abbreviations.

> Shakespeare was born in Stratford-upon-Avon, Warwickshire, United Kingdom, in the 16th century. Between about 1590 and 1613, Shakespeare wrote at least 37 plays and collaborated on several more, which is a great achievement. Many of these plays, for example, *Macbeth* and *Romeo and Juliet*, were especially successful both at court and in the public playhouses. In 1613, Shakespeare retired from the theatre and returned to Stratford-upon-Avon. He died and was buried there in 1616.

____

____

____

____

____

____

5 Cross out any errors in **abbreviations** in the following **formal** text. The errors might be simply incorrect or they might be inappropriate for a formal text. Also cross out words that are commonly abbreviated, but which are written in full here. Rewrite the passage correctly on the lines below.

> The *Bbc Television Shakespeare* is a series of British television adaptations of the plays of William Shakespeare. Transmitted in the U Kingdom, the series spanned seven seasons and thirty-seven episodes. By the end of its run, the series had proved both a TV ratings and financial success. 2Day, the complete set is still a popular collection with ppl, and several eps represent the only non-theatrical production currently available on Digital Versatile Disc. The series was shown in Aus by the Aus Broadcasting Commission (abc).
>
> Adapted from https://en.wikipedia.org/wiki/BBC_Television_Shakespeare

____

____

____

____

____

15

UNIT FIFTEEN

Jasper Jones

Focus
Appropriateness and register; commas (6)

Grammar in use

Text A: this essay extract includes examples of inappropriate register (in **blue** text).

Jasper Jones, by Craig Silvey, **is about** a young boy named Charlie Bucktin who lives in the small Australian town of Corrigan during the 1960s. **He's** approached for help by Jasper Jones, **who's** the town's mixed-race **bad boy**, and the first to be blamed for any kind of trouble. **Basically**, Jasper experiences **nasty** racial prejudice and **unfairness**. In the **story**, Charlie's **new** friendship with Jasper **makes** him question right and wrong, and he comes to the **scary realisation** that the law does not always **give out** justice. **At the end of the day**, **I believe** Silvey **makes us think about** 1960s **ideas** and **whether or not we have changed since then**.

Text B: this text shows the appropriate forms of the errors above.

Jasper Jones, by Craig Silvey, **relates the tale of** a young boy named Charlie Bucktin who lives in the small Australian town of Corrigan during the 1960s. **Charlie is** approached for help by Jasper Jones, **who is** the town's mixed-race **scapegoat**, and the first to be blamed for any kind of trouble. **Jasper constantly** experiences **hurtful** racial prejudice and **injustice**. In the **novel**, Charlie's **unfolding** friendship with Jasper **challenges** him to question right and wrong, and he comes to the **frightening realisation** that the law does not always **uphold** justice. Silvey **encourages the reader to reflect on** 1960s **attitudes and values** and **to consider whether or not they are any different to those that prevail today**.

About grammar

We write differently depending on the context and the type of text—its topic, its purpose and its audience. Written language can vary from extremely **informal** texts, such as a written conversation or emails, to highly **formal** texts, such as essays, reports and journals. It's important that you choose an **appropriate register** (level of language) for the type of text you are creating.

An **informal register** should be **avoided** in academic writing. Three features of an informal register are **personal language, colloquial language** and the use of **figures of speech**.

- **Personal language** is subjective and shows personal opinion. It is shown through the use of **personal pronouns** such as **I**, **we** and **us**; **judgement words** such as **I believe** and *I think*; and **emotive words** such as **nasty** and **scary** in Text A. Although academic writing requires opinion, this opinion needs to be presented as objective and based on sound reason or research. Personal language reduces the power of your argument, making it seem biased and unreasonable.
- **Colloquial language** is language used in conversation or other informal situations. Colloquialisms include **informal expressions** such as **basically**, *you know, a lot, reckon* and *racking my brains*; **contractions** such as *it's, wouldn't* and *can't*; ***abbreviations*** *such as LOL* and *BTW*; and ***slang*** *such as arvo, barbie, freak out, chillax* and *dude*. While it may be acceptable in social emails and texting, colloquial language will reduce the quality of formal written text.

- **Figures of speech** are words or phrases that mean something different from their literal meaning. They are usually **metaphors** or **similes**; for example, *light as a feather* and *climbing the ladder of success.* These may be used in creative writing such as poetry and prose, but they should be **avoided** in academic writing. **Figures of speech** often become **clichés**, which is a term used to describe overused and tired expressions; for example, **At the end of the day** in Text A. A better expression would be *furthermore* or *finally*. Other examples of clichéd figures of speech which should be avoided in academic writing include: *by the same token, time will tell* and *the writing is on the wall.* Clichés do not allow writers to express their ideas in **new** and **fresh** ways and are too **conversational** for academic writing.

A **formal register** is needed in academic writing. Three features of formal register are **technical language**, **nominalisation** and **choice of precise, complex vocabulary**.

- **Technical language** is specialist language associated with the topic or subject you are writing about. The use of technical language increases the authority and formality of your ideas; for example, in Text B, **attitudes and values** (as opposed to ideas) are examples of technical language that relate specifically to your study of English. Other examples of technical language are *digital, server* and *cross-platform* from the field of communications, and *antibiotic, ultrasound* and *immunisation* from the field of medicine.
- **Nominalisation** will help you create a formal, academic tone and write in a general way about issues and ideas rather than about specific individuals, incidents and experiences. Nominalisation is when verbs and adjectives are turned into nouns; for example, **realisation** from *realise* (verb), *difficulty* from *difficult* (adjective), and *reality* from *real* (adjective).

  Nominalisation helps to place the focus on the action or process rather than the person who is involved in it. Look at this example:

  Jasper **realises** *that racial prejudice exists and is confronted by it.* (using the verb *realise*)

  The **realisation** *that racial prejudice exists is confronting for Jasper.* (using the noun *realisation*)
- **Precise, complex vocabulary** rather than general and simple language is needed in academic texts to discuss complex ideas; for example, in Text B **relates the tale of** (rather than **is about**), **scapegoat** (rather than **bad boy**), **injustice** (rather than **unfairness**), **unfolding** (rather than **new**), **challenges** (rather than **makes**), **uphold** (rather than **give out**), **encourages** (rather than **makes**).
- Other aspects of language you should consider in relation to appropriate register are whether the **active or passive voice** is needed (you read about this in Unit 9) and how best to use **modality** to express your ideas (you read about this in Unit 12).

Boost your grammar skills

1 Cross out examples of **personal** or **colloquial** language in the following essay extract.

> *Jasper Jones* is told from the excellent point of view of Charlie, who I think is the main character of the novel. I'm pleased that the book is told from his perspective in the first person and that we are rarely connected to the secret thoughts of other characters, some of whom are creepy. The novel's fun events are mostly shown to the reader through Charlie's perspective. I believe the book is told in chronological order, without any disappointing gaps in the timeline of events.

2 Find a more **formal** alternative for the following **colloquial words** and **expressions**.

For example: I was cheesed off with my friend. not pleased

a I thought he was pulling my leg. ____________

b The job was easier said than done. ____________

c The character was in hot water. ____________

d Are you kidding me? ____________

e He might get the axe unless he starts getting to work on time. ____________

f She's turning into a couch potato. ____________

g I'm not sure that transaction was above board. ____________

3 Underline the **figures of speech** in the following sentences.

a The character of Charlie Bucktin is as solid as a rock and everyone depends upon him in the novel.

b Jasper Jones hopes to fly like an eagle; however, his circumstances do not support his independence.

c Mr Wishart is on a steep learning curve and needs to toe the line or his family will be destroyed.

d Charlie, although believing that every cloud has a silver lining, still needs to think outside the box to solve Jasper's problems.

e Charlie hit the nail on the head with his solution to the problem and said it was a piece of cake.

4 Underline the **figures of speech** in the following sentences, and then rewrite them below using language more suitable for academic texts.

For example:

The time had come to make a decision as the ball was now in Jasper's court.

The time had come to make a decision as Jasper was now in control.

a The character was advised to lift his game or else suffer the consequences.

____

b Eliza is a breath of fresh air who wants to support and care for Charlie.

____

c As Mrs Wishart was feeling under the weather, she was advised to rest.

____

d Jasper was not out of the woods yet and needed to watch his back.

____

e The character needs to get back on track as there are people relying on him to carry the ball.

____

5 Match the correct definition to the following **technical words** and **phrases** used in your study of English.

a allegory	factors that influence the creation of a text and its interpretation
b audience	the categories that texts are grouped by, e.g. sci-fi, western, horror
c composing	an object used to represent something else
d context	the intended group of readers, listeners or viewers
e symbol	a fictional story of events and experiences
f emotive language	a story that has more than one level of meaning
g genre	language that results in an emotional response
h layout	the action of creating written, spoken or visual texts
i narrative	giving human qualities to things, animals and emotions
j personification	the way information is arranged on a page or screen

6 Common **suffixes** used in the **nominalisation** process are *tion, ment* and *ence*. Add one of these to each of the following verbs in order to change them to nouns.

For example: frustrate frustration

a argue ______________ **b** independent ______________

c govern ______________ **d** continue ______________

e nominalise ______________ **f** advance ______________

g persist ______________ **h** inspire ______________

i introduce ______________ **j** promote ______________

k reflect ______________

7 Underline the **nominalisations** in the sentences below. Then rewrite each sentence in less formal everyday speech. Try to keep the complete sense of the sentence.

For example: The technique demonstrates the character's sense of eagerness.

The technique demonstrates that the character is eager.

a The author's depiction of Corrigan is realistic and accurate.

____

b The novel promotes reader involvement.

____

c Humour is used to show the friendly relationship between Charlie and Jeffrey.

____

d The description of characters' lives creates interest for the reader.

____

8 Find a more **precise** and **complex** expression to replace each of the following underlined words and expressions. You may need to use a thesaurus.

a Charles Bucktin is intellectual rather than sporty. ______________

b Charles wants to become a writer, and reads important books during the course of the novel. ______________

c Charlie thinks that Jasper looks a lot older.

---

d Jasper has a bad reputation, but often is blamed for crimes he does not do.

---

e Eliza, Charlie's girlfriend, is described as smart and looks like Audrey Hepburn.

---

f Because of his Vietnamese background, Jeffrey often experiences hate because he is Asian. But he accepts the bad behaviour with good humour.

Punctuation in use

Jasper Jones is a 2009 novel by Australian writer Craig Silvey. **It has won and been shortlisted for several major awards, and was selected by the University of Canberra as its inaugural 'UC Book of the Year' for 2013.**

Protagonist Charlie Bucktin, **a likeable, canny, thick-skinned 13-year-old boy**, lives in the regional mining town of Corrigan. **While he acknowledges that he is somewhat socially awkward, his real problem is being physically uncoordinated in a town that values sporting ability. He is fairly intelligent; however, this causes the other students to resent him. His best friend is Jeffrey Lu, a Vietnamese boy who regularly experiences racial discrimination, and he is always there as support to Charlie.**

On a summer evening in 1965, **Jasper Jones, who is an outcast, visits Charlie and asks for his help**. Jasper takes Charlie to his secret glade in the bush where **Charlie finds the shire president's daughter, Laura Wishart, in a shocking situation.**

About punctuation

So far you have learnt that **commas** help us make our meaning clear by separating the different parts of a sentence. As a general guide, commas may be used where we feel they are needed so that a sentence makes sense.

To review what you have learnt so far, commas separate:

- **items in a list** of three or more; for example, **a likeable, canny, thick-skinned 13-year-old boy**
- **connecting words and expressions** at the start or middle of a sentence such as *however, nevertheless, in fact, similarly* and *conversely*; for example, *You say you won't like the book. I am determined,* **nevertheless**, *to make you read it.*
- **names of people** within sentences; for example, **Charlie finds the shire president's daughter, Laura Wishart, in a shocking situation.**
- **short expressions** like *wow, um, gosh, yes, no, you know* and *please* from the rest of the sentence
- **question tags** such as *will you* or *isn't it* from the rest of the sentence; for example, *It's life and death stuff,* **isn't it**?

- **ending comments** from the rest of the sentence such as *I think, I suppose, I suggest* and *I wonder*; for example, *The book has been reprinted about 10 times,* **I think.**
- **long chunks of extra information** from the rest of the sentence; for example, **His best friend is Jeffrey Lu, a Vietnamese boy who regularly experiences racial discrimination, and he is always there as support to Charlie.**
- **two or more long statements** joined by words such as *and, but* and *or*; for example, **It has won and been shortlisted for several major awards, and was selected by the University of Canberra as its inaugural 'UC Book of the Year' for 2013.**
- **adverbial clauses** at the start of sentences; for example, **While he acknowledges that he is somewhat socially awkward, his real problem is being uncoordinated in a town that values sporting ability.**
- **dependent clauses** within a sentence when that clause adds extra but non-essential information; for example, **Jasper Jones, who is an outcast, visits Charlie and asks for his help.**

Caution!

- If **two independent clauses** are **connected** by a **conjunctive adverb** (sometimes called a **connective**) such as *however, therefore, otherwise, instead* or *nonetheless*, use a **semicolon** or a **full stop**, not a comma. For example, **He is fairly intelligent; however, this causes the other students to resent him** or *He is fairly intelligent. However, this causes the other students to resent him.*
- **Do not place** commas **between subjects and verbs**; for example, *Charlie and Jeffrey and Eliza went to watch the cricket* not *Charlie and Jeffrey and Eliza, went to watch the cricket.*

Boost your punctuation skills

1 Place **semicolons** and/or **commas** in the following sentences that contain conjunctive adverbs. They may contain one or more independent clauses.

- **a** Jasper is forced to hide from Corrigan otherwise he may be targeted by the police.
- **b** Charlie does not reject Jasper's request for help instead he chooses to follow him.
- **c** Eliza meanwhile waits for Charlie at the bookshop as they had planned.
- **d** Charlie is exhausted nonetheless he waits patiently to see if Jasper will arrive.
- **e** Consequently the events cast a shroud of fear over the little town of Corrigan.

2 Use your knowledge to place **commas** in the following paragraphs.

- **a** Charlie's mother Ruth promotes her image as a good mother wife member of the CWA and civic volunteer. She is a demanding and at times difficult mother and she and Charlie appear to have an uneasy relationship. However he does seem to get on with his father very well.
- **b** When Charlie finds his mother in a relationship with a man who is not his father the power balance shifts between them. When this happens Ruth loses her control over Charlie and Charlie learns to redefine his attitudes towards his mother.
- **c** Pete Wishart Laura and Eliza's father is the most aggressive character in the novel. Although he appears to be a man of moral standing the audience learns he is quite the opposite.
- **d** In spite of their own wicked depraved and corrupt behaviour Corrigan's citizens have decided that Jasper Jones is a bad influence. He is often accused of committing a crime despite his protestations even when he was nowhere near the event when it occurred.

e Even though he is a thief Jasper behaves with honour and integrity. Although he is a boy not yet an adult he feels he failed to protect Laura. Charlie tries to uncover what she needed protection from but Jasper keeps her secrets even after she's gone.

3 Use your knowledge to place **commas** in the following paragraph.

> Yes I was there. It was horrific actually. After Jasper got her down I fell into a stupor of disbelief and couldn't believe it was happening. Life's pretty funny isn't it? One day you're coasting along nothing really unusual happens and then you get the fright of your life. This will really change who I am I suppose. I wish I'd never met Jasper Jones left my house or gotten involved you know.

4 Cross out the **commas** which are incorrectly used in the following sentences.

a Like Jasper, Jeffrey Lu's family, is also unwanted and unwelcome.

b Australian men, including those, who are from Corrigan, are drafted to fight in the Vietnam War.

c The Lus, despite being residents of Corrigan, are exposed to ongoing racism, and abuse.

d The Lus try hard, to show their allegiance to Australia, but their attempts are met with contempt.

e Jeffrey is called 'Cong', by the cricket team, a reference to the Viet Cong, and his heritage is mocked.

5 Use all your knowledge of **commas** to punctuate the following paragraphs.

> *Jasper Jones* begins as Charlie Bucktin is approached by Jasper Jones the town trouble-maker who claims to have discovered his girlfriend Laura in a tragic position. Jasper who believes that he will be blamed asks Charlie to promise him not to tell anyone what happened. Although he immediately feels worried Charlie agrees but wants to tell the police. Charlie is terrified however that the police already know of his involvement.
>
> The novel as it unfolds touches on many social moral personal and emotional issues. From a dramatic opening chapter as seen through the eyes of Charlie Bucktin it exposes the life of a country town and reveals its hidden and shady secrets.
>
> Charlie develops over a period of several months from an innocent 13-year-old and sees more of life and its dark side than he really should. The book nonetheless is not all serious. The exchanges between Jeffrey Lu his best mate and a Vietnamese Australian are at times enormously amusing. Even during serious moments Charlie is able to produce a smile from the reader through his honest observations.
>
> The main interaction occurs between Charlie and Jasper Jones a young loner who is ostracised by the people of Corrigan and branded as the local trouble-maker. These two who are bound together by circumstance form a deep bond that will establish their friendship for life.

Revision Test 3

Grammar

Shade one circle to show the correct answer.

1 The following sentence is an example of direct speech:
The student complained, 'Why do I always get chosen first for public speaking?'

Choose the correct indirect speech example of that sentence.

- ◯ The student complained that he always gets chosen first for public speaking.
- ◯ The student complained that he always got chosen first for public speaking.
- ◯ The student complained that he's always getting chosen first for public speaking.

2 The following sentence is an example of indirect speech:

The boy said that he had eaten the whole cake after all.

Choose the correct direct speech example of that sentence:

- ◯ The boy said, 'I've eaten the whole cake after all!'
- ◯ The boy said, 'I ate the whole cake after all!'
- ◯ The boy said, 'I had eaten the whole cake after all!'

3 Which sentence expresses the least certainty?

- ◯ I am very likely to visit him at some stage.
- ◯ I think it could perhaps influence the committee's decision.
- ◯ You must never leave your pets in the car on a hot day.

4 Which verb completes this sentence with the most certain feeling?
You really ________________ go and see the theatre production as it was an excellent version of the book.

◯ should ◯ might ◯ must ◯ ought to

5 Which transition signal should be placed in the following sentence?

Transition signals can create powerful links between ideas and can help your reader understand your ideas. ________________, these words all have different meanings and purposes.

◯ Finally ◯ Therefore ◯ However ◯ Otherwise

6 Which reference pronoun belongs in the following sentence?

By the simplest definition, architecture is the design of buildings, executed by architects. However, ________ is also the expression of thought in building.

◯ who ◯ it ◯ he ◯ they

7 Which synonym is suitable to replace the underlined word in the following sentence?

Steaming beetroot preserves <u>valuable</u> nutrients that are considered ________________ for your health.

◯ precious ◯ respectful ◯ beneficial ◯ positive

8 Which synonym is suitable to replace the underlined word in the following sentence?

The Brothers Grimm created countless folktales in their lifetime. I think *Little Red Riding Hood* is the best they ________________.

◯ formed ◯ invented ◯ produced ◯ shaped

9 Which sentence is ambiguous?

◯ The employees were pleased to hear that they would receive a pay rise.
◯ The owners told the employees that they would receive a pay rise.
◯ 'A pay rise will be given to all employees,' said the owners.

10 Which sentence contains a dangling modifier?

◯ After reading a fantastic book, I'm really looking forward to seeing the film.
◯ After reading a fantastic book, the movie based on it is guaranteed to be thrilling.
◯ After reading a fantastic book, the boy recommended it to his friend.

11 Which sentence contains a dangling modifier?

◯ Hoping to excuse my lateness, my mum wrote a note for my teacher.
◯ Hoping to excuse my lateness, I gave the note from my mum to the teacher.
◯ Hoping to excuse my lateness, the note explained that I had been ill overnight.

In questions 12–14, choose the underlined word that could be removed from each sentence.

12 I was thrilled when the chemist offered me a free gift with my purchase!

◯ thrilled ◯ offered ◯ free ◯ purchase

13 There's an unconfirmed rumour my favourite singer is coming to town.

◯ unconfirmed ◯ rumour ◯ favourite ◯ town

14 I really hope that during the course of your employment we are able to cooperate together effectively.

◯ really ◯ course ◯ cooperate ◯ together

15 Which sentence contains a parallel structure?

◯ They described swimming at the beach, climbing local hills, and a lunch at the local restaurant.
◯ They described a swim at the beach, climbing local hills, and a lunch at the local restaurant.
◯ They described swimming at the beach, climbing local hills, and having lunch at the local restaurant.

16 Which sentence contains a parallel structure?

◯ Tran liked watching movies, to share stories with his friends, and to read a book before bedtime.
◯ Tran liked to watch movies, share stories with his friends, and read a book before bedtime.
◯ Tran liked to watch movies, share stories with his friends, and reading a book before bedtime.

17 Which sentence would be inappropriate in an essay?

- ◯ The character decides to leave home, which is an unfortunate event.
- ◯ I don't like it when the character decides to leave home.
- ◯ The character's decision to leave home influences those around him.

18 Which sentence contains emotive language?

- ◯ I was moved to tears when the old lady was reunited with her child.
- ◯ The old lady reuniting with her son was particularly dramatic.
- ◯ When the old lady was reunited with her son, the reader felt satisfaction.

19 Which sentence contains no colloquial language?

- ◯ Let's crank out the old record player. She's as old as the hills but she'll be right.
- ◯ Let's listen to some old records today during lunch.
- ◯ It would be unreal to hear your old records again during lunch.

20 Which sentence would be inappropriate in an essay?

- ◯ The character is driven by revenge and works tirelessly until it is exacted.
- ◯ The character really burns the midnight oil in her attempt to seek revenge.
- ◯ The character is overwhelmed by revenge and works hard to achieve it.

21 Which sentence shows the best use of technical language?

- ◯ The student told the class what happened during her school trip to Tibet.
- ◯ The student recounted what happened during her school trip to Tibet.
- ◯ The student talked about what happened during her school trip to Tibet.

22 Which of the following underlined words is a nominalisation?

The author <u>supports</u> the <u>representation</u> of his character as <u>necessary</u> to the <u>story</u>.

◯ supports ◯ representation ◯ necessary ◯ story

23 Which of the following underlined words is a nominalisation?

The <u>investigation</u> <u>concluded</u> that the <u>driver</u> was not to blame for the <u>accident</u>.

◯ investigation ◯ concluded ◯ driver ◯ accident

Punctuation

1 The following sentence is an example of indirect speech:

The teacher said that this student's essay was very well structured.

Choose the correctly punctuated direct speech example of that sentence.

- ◯ The teacher said 'This student's essay is very well structured.'
- ◯ The teacher said, 'This student's essay is very well structured'.
- ◯ The teacher said, 'This student's essay is very well structured.'

2 The following sentence is an example of direct speech:
The politician explained, 'We want to end the burden of debt for students.'
Choose the correctly punctuated indirect speech example of that sentence.

- ◯ The politician explained that they wanted to end the burden of debt for students.
- ◯ The politician 'explained that they wanted to end the burden of debt for students.'
- ◯ The politician explained that they wanted to 'end the burden' of debt for students.

3 Which underlined word should be enclosed by single quotation marks?

Dad's <u>favourite</u> song is <u>Delilah</u> by Tom <u>Jones</u>. He's so <u>uncool</u>.

◯ ◯ ◯ ◯

4 Which sentence is correct?

- ◯ Its plain to see that she has natural writing talent.
- ◯ It's been so wonderful to see her writing develop.
- ◯ The story she's been writing is really interesting—its over there if you'd like to read it.

5 Which word correctly fills the gap in the following sentence?

The gallery owners were asked to return the painting as it was never ______________ in the first place.

◯ there's ◯ they'res ◯ their's ◯ theirs

6 Which sentence is correct?

- ◯ The teacher would've handed back their essays but there wasn't time.
- ◯ The teacher would've handed back there essays but there wasn't time.
- ◯ The teacher woul'dve handed back their essays but there was'nt time.

7 Which sentence is punctuated correctly?

- ◯ The school's rules were clear: no one would have access to their devices during the day.
- ◯ The school's rules were clear (no one would have access to their devices during the day).
- ◯ The school's rules were clear—no one—would have access to their devices during the day.

8 Which sentence uses the semicolon correctly?

- ◯ While visiting Vienna in 1781; Mozart was dismissed from his Salzburg position. He chose to stay in the capital, where he achieved fame but little financial security.
- ◯ While visiting Vienna in 1781, Mozart was dismissed from his Salzburg position; he chose to stay in the capital, where he achieved fame but little financial security.
- ◯ While visiting Vienna in 1781, Mozart was dismissed from his Salzburg position and he chose to stay in the capital; where he achieved fame but little financial security.

9 Which sentence has been abbreviated correctly?

- ◯ A delegate from the UN is a VIP, although they do require ID in order to verify themselves.
- ◯ We are looking for a MoC for our wedding business. Please check our FAC page to see if you are suitable.
- ◯ According to SbS news, we need to change our clocks tonight, so the AEST will change.

10 Which is an appropriate abbreviation for the underlined word?

The Governor of NSW will visit our school to open the new building.

◯ Gov ◯ Gv. ◯ Gov. ◯ Gr

In questions 11–15, which sentence is correctly punctuated?

11
◯ Author Tim Winton was born in Karrinyup, Western Australia, but moved at the age of 12 to Albany.
◯ Author Tim Winton was born in Karrinyup Western Australia but moved at the age of 12 to Albany.
◯ Author Tim Winton was born in Karrinyup Western Australia, but moved at the age of 12 to Albany.

12
◯ Winton has lived in Italy France Ireland and Greece but he currently lives in Fremantle, near Perth, with his wife and three children.
◯ Winton has lived in Italy, France, Ireland, and Greece but he currently lives in Fremantle near Perth with his wife and three children.
◯ Winton has lived in Italy, France, Ireland and Greece, but he currently lives in Fremantle, near Perth, with his wife and three children.

13
◯ While at university Winton wrote his first novel, *An Open Swimmer* which won The Vogel Literary Award in 1981, launching his writing career.
◯ While at university Winton wrote his first novel, *An Open Swimmer*, which won The Vogel Literary Award in 1981 launching his writing career.
◯ While at university, Winton wrote his first novel, *An Open Swimmer*, which won The Vogel Literary Award in 1981, launching his writing career.

14
◯ It wasn't until *Cloudstreet* was published in 1991, however, that his writing career was properly established.
◯ It wasn't until, *Cloudstreet,* was published in 1991, however, that his writing career was properly established.
◯ It wasn't until *Cloudstreet* was published in 1991; however, that his writing career was properly established.

15
◯ His novel *Breath*, was published in 2008. His latest novel is *Eyrie* published in 2013.
◯ His novel *Breath* was published in 2008. His latest novel is *Eyrie*, published in 2013.
◯ His novel, *Breath* was published in 2008. His latest novel is *Eyrie*, published in 2013.

Answers

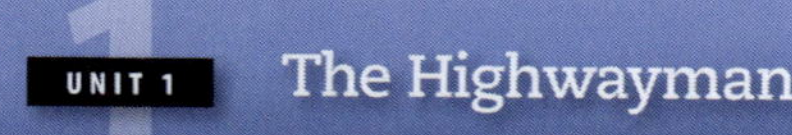

UNIT 1 The Highwayman

Grammar pages 2–4

1 He did not come in the dawning; he did not come at noon;
And out of the tawny sunset, before the rise of the moon,
When the road was a gypsy's ribbon, looping the purple moor,
A red-coat troop came marching—
Marching—marching—
King George's men came marching, up to the old inn-door.

2 'The Highwayman' is a narrative poem written by Alfred Noyes, first published in 1906. The following year it was included in Noyes's collection, *Forty Singing Seamen and Other Poems*, becoming an immediate success. The poem, set in 18th-century rural England, tells the story of an unnamed highwayman who is in love with Bess, a landlord's daughter. Betrayed to the authorities by Tim, a jealous ostler, the highwayman escapes ambush when Bess sacrifices her life to warn him. Learning of her death, he dies in a futile attempt at revenge, shot down on the highway. In the final stanza, the ghosts of the lovers meet again on winter nights.

3
- **a** On one level, the poem is a description of a windy night and the highwayman's approach on horseback.
- **b** There is a strong connection with stormy waters, as seen in 'a torrent of darkness' and 'cloudy seas'.
- **c** The poet's creation of the world seems oddly unsettled and even the moon itself seems unstable—it is 'tossed' about in the sky.
- **d** Instrumental to the poem is the association of the highwayman with the chaotic and mysterious forces of nature.

4 **a** stable-wickets **b** shutters **c** blood **d** skies **e** sweat **f** madness **g** hay **h** moonlight **i** curses **j** darkness **k** kisses **l** feet **m** dark **n** hooves/hoofs **o** breaths

5
- **a** A painting of *The Highwayman* is in the national gallery. **N**
- **b** I'm enjoying tonight's poetry reading. **V**
- **c** The poem *The Highwayman* has a fantastic ending. **N**
- **d** The meeting of the two lovers was doomed from the start. **N**
- **e** The 'ghostly galleon' was tossing over the night sky. **V**
- **f** Bess was waiting for the highwayman's return. **V**

6
- **a** his whip on the shutters
- **b** the yellow gold before the morning light
- **c** the black cascade of perfume
- **d** its waves in the moonlight
- **e** the tawny sunset,
- **f** the rise of the moon
- **g** the stroke of midnight

Punctuation pages 4–5

1
- **a** A melodic effect can be achieved from poetic techniques such as assonance, alliteration, onomatopoeia and rhythm.
- **b** In our modern society, a variety of cultures and languages influence poetic forms, styles and techniques.
- **c** Visual images, word association and a language's musical qualities influence how a poem is created.
- **d** Different types of meter played key roles in Classical Early European Eastern and Modern poetry.
- **e** The line, couplet, stanza and verse paragraph form the main elements of a poem's structure.

2 The development of auditory skills comes from listening to poems and songs. While you read, sing, play and act out poems you are learning that sounds make words and that words can be fun, amusing and enjoyable.

3 **a** Reading poetry offers joy, excitement and insight to both new and inexperienced readers.
b The act of creating poetry strengthens individuals, including realisations about who you are, what you think, what your life has been like, what you want, and what you want to accomplish.
c People write poetry through a desire to share, promote education, or be inspirational.
d Poetry can be publicly recognised by sharing, reading, posting or publishing.
e People who write poetry may become more sensitive to larger issues in life, feel connected, and develop an appreciation of life.

4 **a** 'Poetry is what in a poem makes you laugh, cry, prickle, be silent, makes your toe nails twinkle, makes you want to do this or that or nothing, makes you know that you are alone in the unknown world.' Dylan Thomas
b 'The poet's mind is in fact a receptacle for seizing and storing up numberless feelings, phrases and images, which remain there until all the particles which can unite to form a new compound are present together.' TS Eliot
c 'There are three things that a poem must reach: the eye, the ear, and what we may call the heart or the mind. It is most important of all to reach the heart of the reader.' Robert Frost
d 'Use no superfluous word, no adjective, which does not reveal something.' Ezra Pound
e 'Poetry is simply the most beautiful, impressive and widely effective mode of saying things, and hence its importance.' Matthew Arnold

UNIT 2 Jane Eyre

Grammar pages 7–9

1 **a** boy, you **b** interruption, that **c** moonlight, this **d** John Reed, whom

2 her, she, Her, She, It, us

3 **a** you, **S** **b** I, **S** **c** he, **S**; him, **O** **d** me, **O** **e** you; us, **S** and **O**

4 **a** her **b** hers **c** his **d** her, theirs, hers **e** our

5 **a** What **b** Who **c** Who **d** whom **e** Whose **f** Which

6 **a** are **b** are **c** is, other **d** has, its **e** is, it

7 Few are able to disagree that *Jane Eyre* is a classic novel. The story begins with Jane as a girl alone but with a defiant spirit. She slowly changes into an intelligent young woman who is fiercely independent. Throughout her story, Jane is met with hostility from those around her, often because of problems resulting from low social class. However, when Jane meets Rochester, both are immediately attracted to the other. Everyone is opposed to the match, yet Jane maintains her independent spirit.

Punctuation pages 10–11

1 **a** The only time Jane, the book's protagonist, truly feels ready to make a decision is after she has consulted her own personal, moral compass.
b In addition, Mr Rochester becomes lame and blind after the fire that ripped through his home.
c 'Don't be afraid, Jane, I saw it was an accident.'
d The novel, however, also discloses that Brontë considered Victorian society patriarchal.
e While the dominant characters present in Jane's life throughout the novel all try, in a variety of ways, to control her, she is largely resistant.
f 'How dare you affirm that, Jane Eyre?'

2 **a** The main journey in *Jane Eyre* is Jane's search for love, for feelings of belonging and family.
b Nevertheless, Jane's quest is continually strengthened by her desire for freedom.
c We meet her as an orphan, who is preoccupied with wanting to reinforce her worth and realise happiness.
d While she does not receive any real love from Mrs Reed, Jane does find other women to form relationships with in the novel.
e In the novel, men such as Mr Rochester, her Uncle John and St John are able easily to make decisions for themselves.

3 **c** However, in not following a path of conformity, Jane challenges convention, and this does reveal the distinctive features of a heroine. ✗

e *Jane Eyre* is often referred to as the earliest notable feminist novel, although in the book there are no themes relating to political, legal, educational or intellectual equality between the sexes. ✗

4 Jane's independence continues to show through. She does not enjoy Rochester smothering her in money, clothes and attention. She is, in fact, fearful that they will change her personal values and morals. She tries to resist. 'I would as soon see you Mr Rochester tricked out in stage-trappings as myself clad in a court-lady's robe.' Furthermore, Jane declares that until she is married to Mr Rochester she will continue to be Adèle's governess and earn her usual wage. This information, which may surprise some readers, further demonstrates Jane's desire to prioritise her independence.

UNIT 3 A cycling experience

Grammar pages 13–15

1
- a has created
- b was knocked
- c went, suggested, needed
- d recommended, knew, would find
- e would cycle, could, was
- f could evolve, loves, pleases

2 a had b would, may c does d should have e will

3 a A b A c P d P e P

4 b, e

5 a is b remember c were d like e is

6 **Why cycle Japan?** Japan is a beautiful country to explore by bicycle. The countryside is sparsely populated with little traffic, but still offers a strong cycling infrastructure. There are numerous unexpected country back roads, and many of those are tarsealed and comfortable to ride. Japanese drivers are very courteous. The diversity of food, culture, history and natural environment is so interesting that most people will return to Japan.

7 a had been b had Iwasaki been cycling c has spent d had seen e will have

8 saw, climbed, had experienced, saw, have been crying, will begin, will be saving

Punctuation page 16

1
- a Hey, I wanted to tell you about what happened during my trip.
- b He's had an amazing journey, hasn't he?
- c Goodness gracious, nearly getting married was the event that most scared me!
- d You know, I would love to hear more about your trip.
- e You won't be staying long in India, will you?

2 Hi, my name is Keiichi [,] Iwasaki. I am a Japanese man who is travelling around the world. You might see me riding past on my bike [,] or working as a street performer. I need to entertain people to earn a living. My travel started, I think, about nine years ago. Through this journey I would like to learn how we can make the world [,] a better place. Support me, please!

3
- c I mean, really, how hard could the ride be, right? It ended up being pretty hard. I got sick during the first week and woke up every night with a hacking cough for 10 days.
- d Lastly, you become a machine. You are a pair of legs, a pair of lungs and a stomach that never fills.

4
- a I was worried when the instructor said, 'Come here Alina', but she just wanted to remind me about the competition.
- b When beginning training you should warm up, do a mixed-intensity workout and then cool down.
- c Stop every 10 to 20 kilometres, depending on your ability. Consume some water, eat some food and check your bike for any problems.
- d Warm up and stretch for 10 minutes. Star jumps, jogging on the spot and various leg stretches work best. This will avoid cramps in the legs, especially thighs.
- e Generally speaking, beginning with a short ride, even around the block, will get you started.

5 How to pack for such a trip, Henry? I suggest that, since we will also be taking the train, we should not bring bike luggage, spare parts or load ourselves down. Do you know anyone else who has done a biking trip like this in Japan and, if so, could you ask them for some recommendations? I am inclined to pack my normal rolling suitcase, adapt to bike travel as needed, and see how we go. We will certainly come equipped with raincoats, rain pants and wet weather gear. I mean, we're used to doing that at home! It's going to be tricky, isn't it?

UNIT 4 Animal Farm

Grammar pages 18–20

1 **a** given **b** crept **c** been, was **d** caught **e** lain, lost

2 **a** began **b** bitten/bit **c** blew **d** dreamt **e** drank **f** driven **g** forgave **h** gone **i** grew **j** hanged/hung **k** known **l** seen **m** wore

3 **a** arisen **b** flung **c** become **d** built **e** grown **f** begun

4 **a** held **I** **b** accepted **R** **c** provided **R** **d** known **I** **e** quit **I**

5 **a** Clover **b** Mollie **c** people and societies **d** poor burdened workers **e** *Animal Farm*

6 **a** are **b** fled, settled **c** will live, sleep, wear, drink, smoke, touch, engage **d** were, had

7 **a** wants **b** are **c** needs, take **d** loves, are **e** rebel, remove

Punctuation pages 21–22

1
- **a** The revolution in *Animal Farm*, like other revolutions in history, was initiated by a powerful desire for change.
- **b** Aspects of *Animal Farm* that are historically linked to Soviet history, such as the revolution and the failings of the government, are presented symbolically throughout the novel.
- **c** With one accord, though nothing of the kind had been planned beforehand, they flung themselves upon their tormentors.
- **d** Word had spread among the animals during the day that Old Major, an old and respected prize boar, had a strange dream and wanted to speak to them.
- **e** The owners of the farms next door to Animal Farm, including Mr Pilkington of Foxwood and Mr Frederick of Pinchfield, are concerned that the revolution might spread to their own farms.

2
- **a** The animals believe life on the farm has improved to some extent, but they have less food than ever.
- **b** Clover made a sort of wall round them with her great foreleg, and the ducklings nestled down inside it, then promptly fell asleep.
- **c** Snowball tells Mollie she shouldn't want sugar and ribbons, so she tries hard to give them up.
- **d** At the meeting everyone is allowed to voice their opinions and vote, but only the pigs seem to be allowed to make any changes.
- **e** The other animals grumble, but Squealer explains that the pigs are crucial to the running of the farm and they need the milk and apples to stay healthy.

3
- **a** Before leaving, the animals demolished the food.
- **b** To Frederick, Pilkington appeared confident in reaching a compromise.
- **c** Everybody they thought would win, won.
- **d** Animals who can, take advantage of those inferior to them.

4
- **a** The pigs, despite being the greediest, instruct the other animals.
- **e** Now, comrades, what is the nature of this life of ours?

5 The animals of Manor Farm had always been oppressed under the management of Mr Jones. They grow to accept their situation as part of the natural order of life, but it is Old Major, a prize-winning boar, who shares his desire for change with the other animals. It is three young pigs, called Snowball, Napoleon and Squealer, who transform Old Major's dream into a political ideology called Animalism. Initially, the pigs supervise the farming work and all the animals work hard, but there are worrying signs that the pigs distinguish themselves as different from the other animals. The promises of free time, heat or machinery to help never eventuate.

UNIT 5 Mother India

Grammar pages 24–26

1
- **a** India contains many official languages, and locals (over there) speak regional dialects.
- **b** You should visit a silk factory (while) you are there.
- **c** The religious temple in Mysore (rightly) insists that you remove footwear before entering.
- **d** Sacred cows and other different animals (frequently) roam some temple grounds.

e Bumpy rickshaw rides and long-haul flights from Australia can (really) affect your nerves.

2 **a** Our visit to India will be an absolute **adventure**. **emphasising**
b A variety of religions help shape the region's diverse **culture**. **qualitative**
c The Indian **subcontinent** is identified by its commercial and cultural **wealth**. **classifying**
d An open-minded approach is needed when travelling to new and different **places**. **qualitative**
e We had a brilliant and awesome **experience** in India! **emphasising**
f These **suitcases** will be heavy by the end of our journey. **demonstrative**
g Several **acquaintances** have travelled to India and their **trip** was also enjoyable. **quantitative and possessive**

3

Manner	Degree	Place	Time
quietly	very	outside	usually
fast	much	here	yesterday
honestly	almost	over there	once
cheerfully	completely	below	often
well	quite	everywhere	a few months ago

4 **a** Algebra, trigonometry and calculus originally (came) from India.
b There are about 1.6 million people happily (employed) by Indian Railway.
c In the last 1000 years, India has never (invaded) another country.
d Yoga has its origins in India and has (existed) constantly for 5000 years.
e India is considered a very (exciting) travel destination.

5 (suggested answers)
a quickly, promptly **b** hysterically, softly
c awkwardly, hastily **d** dutifully, steadily
e hungrily, well **f** erectly, nervously
g very, enormously **h** finally, deservedly

6 **a** mysteriously **b** terribly
c fully **d** inexpensively
e angrily **f** thankfully
g truly **h** easily

7 **a** This journey is more interesting (interesting) than the one I took last year.
b That was the best (good) train trip I have ever experienced.
c Calcutta was even more fascinating (fascinating) than Bangladesh.
d I finished planning my itinerary faster (fast) than my companions.
e That hotel was the most expensive (expensive) in the entire region.

8 **a** well, adverb **b** good, adjective
c badly, adverb **d** bad, adjective
e tightly, adverb **f** tight, adjective
g quickly, adverb **h** quick, adjective
i really, adverb **j** real, adjective

Punctuation pages 27–28

1 **a** A popular Indian film is *The Legend of Bhagat Singh*.
b The High Court is located on Strand Road.
c The financial hub is home to the Calcutta Stock Exchange.
d Among Calcutta's smaller communities are Chinese, Tamils, Armenians and Greeks.
e Mother Teresa of Calcutta was awarded the Nobel Peace Prize in 1979.
f The Black Hole of Calcutta was a small dungeon in the old Fort William.

2 **a** Bankim chandra chattopadhyay was one of the earliest bengali novelists.
b The Calcutta book Fair is an annual fair showcasing local books.
c the Indian museum houses large collections that showcase indian natural history and Indian art.
d The government college of art and Craft was founded in 1864.
e the academy of fine Arts and other art galleries hold regular art exhibitions.

3 **a** Autumn
b Singh, Summer Olympics
c A, Mayor Chattergee, Kolkata
d September, October
e Bay

4 **a** ✓ **b** ✗ **c** ✓ **d** ✗

5 Many people have asked me what draws me to Kolkata, and it's a difficult question to answer. I received a book with daily quotes from the Blessed Teresa of Calcutta called 'The Joy in Loving'. I remember reading one entry which described a young girl visiting Kolkata from Paris. As soon as I finished school, I decided I would go to Kolkata to volunteer. It was many miles away from my all-girls school in rural England. I began working in a dispensary and led a group of volunteers painting the park at Shishu Bhavan. Since that first visit, I have volunteered elsewhere with the Missionaries of Charity.

Revision Test 1

Grammar pages 29–31

1. compost
2. puppy
3. pyramid
4. the finest green patterned silk
5. her
6. his
7. cat
8. Both are going to make it, but they're going to be late.
9. themselves
10. will have
11. will be looking
12. We would have booked
13. Millions of people all over the world have read the book.
14. bought
15. to learn
16. [the first] studying
17. Singing three songs and playing the piano at the end-of-year concert.
18. The coffee here is better than the coffee from Paul Street.
19. The boy had drunk too much lemonade and was feeling ill as a result.
20. Each of them gets a trophy for winning the premiership.
21. safely
22. already
23. often
24. everywhere
25. As soon as we receive your payment, we will ship the parcel to you.
26. My book was better than yours.
27. I asked the driver to get there quickly.

Punctuation pages 31–32

1. The house looked huge, dark, isolated and scary in the moonlight.
2. There were no people, animals, cars or houses anywhere to be seen.
3. Some people think you should finish school, go to university, travel, and then think about getting a job.
4. The package, small and compact, fit neatly into his back pocket.
5. I know, in fact, she left the country early this morning.
6. Listen to me, Henry, when I'm talking to you!
7. Would you mind passing me the sugar, please?
8. You will be there for my party, won't you?
9. The test won't be as easy the next time, I suppose.
10. The poem, written during the late 19th century, remains popular today.
11. The student knew she had completed all the work necessary, and that the assignment was placed neatly in her bag.
12. Ballarat is a city located on the Yarrowee River and the lower western plains of the Great Dividing Range in the state of Victoria, Australia.
13. Helen Clark, as Prime Minister of New Zealand, served three terms from 1999 to 2008.
14. The Winter Olympics were held in Calgary in 2010.
15. Malala Yousafzai, from Pakistan, was announced as the co-recipient of the 2014 Nobel Peace Prize.

UNIT 6 Renewable energy resources

Grammar pages 34–35

1. **a** S **b** C **c** S **d** C **e** S **f** S
2. **a** ✔ **b** ✘ **c** ✘ **d** ✔ **e** ✘ **f** ✘ **g** ✔
3.
   - **a** Operate the appliance each week and then test it.
   - **b** Buy an efficient refrigerator or you will regret it.
   - **c** Lights and television use electrical energy so you should turn them off.
   - **d** Recycling has many benefits and reduces the amount of paper in landfills yet there are still many trees lost.
   - **e** Renewable sources are either carbon neutral or they do not produce greenhouse gases and so they are much less harmful to the environment.
4. **a** but/yet **b** or **c** and/yet **d** or **e** but/yet
5. **a** or **b** and **c** but **d** nor **e** but
6. **a** No noun/pronoun **b** it **c** it **d** they **e** you

7 **a** subject **b** object **c** subject **d** verb **e** verb **f** object **g** subject

8 Renewable energy is healthy and environmentally friendly and it can be used without depleting the environment. All forms of energy are expensive, but as time and technologies progress, renewable energy generally gets cheaper and fossil fuels generally get more expensive. There are ways to save energy. Open the curtains and use the sunlight instead of turning on the lights, and turn off the dishwasher right before the drying cycle. Let the dishes air dry. There are a lot more ways to save energy and so it's important that everyone pitches in to conserve energy.

Punctuation pages 36–37

1
- **a** Clean energy doesn't emit carbon dioxide (CO_2).
- **b** Solar energy is renewable (this means that energy from the sun never ends).
- **c** Charles F Brush (1849–1929) invented the world's first automatically operated wind turbine.
- **d** Renewable energy uses natural resources that can be renewed (replaced) without harming the environment.
- **e** Polyethylene terephthalate (PET) has a wide range of uses including synthetic fibres and containers for food, beverage and other liquids.

2
- **a** The topic of alternative energy encompasses a range of sub-topics—wind, water, nuclear and geothermal energy.
- **b** Many items in my home require electricity to run—TV set, microwave oven, electric kettle, computer and refrigerator.
- **c** When the sun shines— and we hope it does!— it can heat the water and cool the house.
- **d** The average person is said to throw away—I can't believe it—almost two kilograms of rubbish every day.
- **e** There are a number of ways to become more environmentally friendly— recycle, conserve water and fuel and make other choices that lessen your impact on the environment.

3
- **a** Another form of geothermal energy is called hot rock (this is where water is pumped below the surface to areas of hot rock).
- **b** A landfill site (also known as a tip, dump, rubbish dump or dumping ground) is a site for the disposal of waste materials by burial.
- **c** The term windmill comes from 'to mill' (meaning 'to grind'.)
- **d** Charles F Brush (inventor of the wind turbine) was raised on a farm about seven kilometres from Cleveland, Ohio.
- **e** The gas generated by landfill as it rots is another form of renewable (or 'green') energy.

4
- **a** Solar photovoltaic (PV) technology generates electricity from sunlight.
- **c** Windmills are used in many countries—US, India, Germany and France.

5 Many people are saving money on their power bills by changing from incandescent light bulbs to light-emitting diode (LED) lights. These lights can be used everywhere such as in traffic signals, home lighting and—amazingly—even in eyelashes and bionic contact lenses. LED lights have an extremely long life span (about 50 000 hours) and use much less energy than incandescent bulbs. Switching to LED lighting can save a great deal (40 to 70 per cent). LED was invented by Nick Holonyak, Jr (born 1928) while working as a consulting scientist at General Electric Company (GEC). Holonyak said in *Reader's Digest* (1963) that 'His [Holonyak's] LED would replace Thomas Edison's light bulb.'

UNIT 7 Aesop's Fables

Grammar pages 39–41

1
- **a** that couldn't possibly be his own.
- **b** that Aesop lived during the sixth century BC, although no one knows for sure.
- **c** while king
- **d** because they were short
- **e** because the people were not appreciative enough of the gift, that was given to them by King Croesus

2 **a** compound **b** complex **c** complex **d** compound-complex **e** compound-complex

3 **a** Although **b** While **c** until **d** If **e** Whenever

4 (suggested answers)

- **a** Before this year's English class, I had never read any of *Aesop's Fables*.
- **b** *Aesop's Fables* is important to read, since they give information about ways to behave.
- **c** After reading a fable, you might learn something of importance.
- **d** Whenever I read a fable, I always feel interested.
- **e** While reading, I always wonder what happens next.

5
- **a** that were written by Aesop, defining
- **b** which was translated into Latin in the 13th century, non-defining
- **c** who studied Aesop, defining
- **d** whose theme was human vanity, non-defining
- **e** that life is no better in the city than in the country, defining

6
- **a** Aesop, who may have been born in Ethiopia, spent much of his life living in Greece at the court of King Croesus.
- **b** Fables that are used to teach children morals often pass into our culture as myths and legends.
- **c** The medieval fable was a lengthy animal story that contained a hero.
- **d** A gardener who offers Aesop a basket of vegetables gives it to him as a reward.
- **e** Aesop, whose fables provide great entertainment, is known for stories that are all fairly short.

7
- **a** 2, 3, 1
- **b** 3, 1, 2 or 2, 3, 1
- **c** 2, 1, 3 or 3, 2, 1

8 Fables are short stories that illustrate a particular moral and teach a lesson to children. Fables often feature animals who act and talk like humans and who retain their animal characteristics. *Aesop's Fables* are very entertaining since they are short. They keep children's attention since they feature familiar animals. Although *Aesop's Fables* have been around a long time, they are still popular.

Punctuation page 42

1
- **a** Unless you plan on reading that book on holiday, you shouldn't borrow it.
- **b** When the school bell rang, the students left the classroom.
- **c** After you have finished reading the novel, your assignment is to write a report.
- **d** While some people prefer to read non-fiction, others enjoy fiction and narratives.
- **e** Since we have started learning about fables, we will also be exploring parables.

2
- **a** A fable, which is a story meant to teach a moral lesson, is a type of fictional narrative.
- **b** The characters in a fable, who we like to read about, are usually animals.
- **c** The name Aesop, which means Ethiopia, is derived from the Greek word *Aethiop*.
- **d** Aesop, who many believe lived on a Greek island called Samos, was a slave.
- **e** Parables or allegories, where a moral is usually added, can be seen in most of Aesop's stories.

3
- **a** Some of the best-known fables that are still read to children today are those attributed to Aesop.
- **b** Many of the fables, which include a moral, are well known today
- **c** William Caxton, who was a translator, first printed *Aesop's Fables* in English in 1484.
- **d** A popular fable that is modern is George Orwell's *Animal Farm*.
- **e** Fables, which focused on exposing human weaknesses, became popular in 17th-century France.

4 Aesop, who is credited with the authorship of fables, was a slave. Many believed he lived in Samos, which is a Greek island in the eastern Aegean Sea, but others say he came from Ethiopia. One tradition holds that he came from Thrace, while a later one claims he is Phrygian. The name of his first owner was Xanthus, who was a philosopher, although it is believed that Aesop was eventually freed. Generally speaking, many of his fables are characterised by animals and inanimate objects that speak, solve problems, and who generally have human characteristics.

UNIT 8 Chinese goldminers in Australia

Grammar pages 44–46

1
- **a** He reached the goldfields across the paddock in time for work.
- **b** He got a job for his friend from school.
- **c** I will meet him at the mines at lunchtime instead of at home.

d You need to see the man with the blue shirt with regard to work.

e The workers on the minefields took breaks by the creek.

f The men feel sore from digging in the ground along the ridge.

2 a Chinese miners used different mining methods to the Europeans.

b Chinese workers usually operated as a group and they didn't mix with the general population of the goldfields.

c Seven thousand Chinese people came to work at the Araluen goldfields in southern NSW.

d Chinese miners often worked in groups of 30 to 100 men under the direction of a leader.

e Conflict stemmed from resentment of Chinese successes on the goldfields.

f They found gold missed by Caucasian miners in their haste.

3 a The Chinese are said to have rarely worked in new areas, preferring to go to areas discarded by the Europeans.

b Some Chinese felt duty-bound to seek a better future for their families who remained at home in China.

c Most Chinese men wore their hair in the form of a pigtail which, together with their unique clothes and manner of travelling, often drew contempt from Europeans.

d In the early days of Chinese settlement in Victoria the centre of the Chinese community was in the goldfields.

e Most of the early Chinese immigrants wanted to return to the land of their ancestors and later many did.

4 a verb **b** noun **c** noun **d** noun

e noun and noun

5 a In Australia, the gold rush had a significant impact on the formation of the Australian identity.

b In any discussion of our history, the diggers' rebelliousness and contempt for those in charge during this time remains a central theme.

c In a waterhole near Bathurst, Edward Hargraves discovered a 'grain of gold' and became a legend.

d As a result of the discovery, there was a dramatic change within Australian society.

6 a Only a small minority of Chinese people were able to pay for their own voyage and migrate to Australia free of debt.

b They were often forced to move to new areas or made to work on empty sites.

c The government tried to award basic rights to the Chinese and provided them with improved legal access.

d Many Chinese migrants left the colony for other states or returned to China.

e It was common for Chinese to be removed from areas where gold had been discovered.

7 The Chinese diggers moved from goldfield to goldfield within NSW and across the border. Their presence and experience are shown from the observations of Anglo-Australians, from archaeological digs and from objects saved by families and community members. There are few written accounts and sources from a Chinese perspective. The Chinese attracted particular attention and local newspapers were quick to comment on their diligence, tirelessness and productivity. Admiration of their work ethic was offset by envy and resentment.

Punctuation pages 47–48

1 a 'There is no doubt that the gold rushes had a huge effect on our development as a nation,' said the teacher.

b 'Do you know where the first grain of gold was discovered?' asked Kamal.

c 'You must make sure you visit Ballarat when you drive through Victoria!' insisted Mrs Morrison.

d Hargraves said: 'The similarity in geological features between the Australian and Californian goldfields boded well for the search of gold in Australia.'

e 'There has been a universal rush to the diggings,' the commissioner stated.

2 a 'Did you know that the 1850s also saw the construction of the first railway?' Maria said.

b 'Why would the new convict arrivals want to work for a living when a fortune awaited them on the goldfields?' asked our history teacher.

c 'We swear by the Southern Cross to stand truly by each other, and fight to defend our rights and liberties,' said miners at the Eureka Stockade.

d 'Eureka!' shouted the miner as he struck a pocket of gold.

e 'Modern ideas about goldfield life ignore the filth, greed, crime, selfishness and racism that were actually very common,' stated the historian.

3 **a** 'When finds of wondrous treasure set all the south ablaze,' wrote Henry Lawson, 'and you and I were faithful mates all through the roaring days.'
b 'Today I learnt that 40 000 Chinese made their way to Australia,' said Tobias. 'In 1861, Chinese immigrants made up 3.3 per cent of the Australian population.'
c 'The gold rush brought to Australia people with a range of skills and professions,' said the lecturer, 'and this was unthought-of prior to the discovery of gold.'
d 'Life was difficult for the Chinese in Australia,' explained the historian. 'In exchange for their passage money, they worked on the goldfields until their debt was paid off.'

4 **a** The authorities said, 'The Chinese were known as untiring workers and that's why there was so much jealousy.'
b The students asked, 'Why didn't anybody step in to help the Chinese goldminers during the attack?'
c I exclaimed to my friends, 'I am so shocked at the violence exhibited towards Asian goldminers!'

5 'Our money and property were plundered,' said Lum Khen Yang. 'We had not the means of purchasing a morsel to put into our mouths and there appeared no way by which we could extricate ourselves from poverty.' Yang continued: 'But then we heard intelligence regarding a new goldfield in an English colony.'

'We were told that men from all parts of the world were congregated there,' Yang explained, 'that the people were peaceably disposed, and that the country abounded in everything.'

'The idea of going to such a country was delightful!' he exclaimed.

UNIT 9 Social learning

Grammar pages 50–51

1 **a** A **b** P **c** P **d** A **e** A **f** P

2 **a** Young people established the young adult group.
b The Principal will reveal the results next Friday.
c A company in China manufactured the equipment.
d Socially isolated young adults can learn new skills.
e Team leaders present real-life experiences throughout the program.

3 **a** can build, **active**
b are strengthened, **passive**
c is considered, **passive**
d learn, **active**
e is judged, **passive**

4 **a** teenagers **b** NA **c** NA **d** all teachers **e** NA

5 **a** ✔ **b** ✘ **c** ✔ **d** ✘

6 **a** ✔ **b** ✔ **c** ✘ **d** ✘

7 Social awareness (involve) involves two key areas. Firstly, it is an awareness that social problems (face) are faced regularly by individuals and communities. Secondly, it (to be) is the ability to sympathise with an individual's thoughts and feelings and to realise that individuals (impact) are impacted by wider forces within their community. Social awareness (promote) promotes respectful relationships and encourages skills that (create) are created by emotions and responsible decision-making.

Punctuation pages 52–53

1 **a** Teachers', student's **b** one's **c** people's **d** Learners' **e** Students', teacher's

2 **a** Louisa and Antonio's teacher is teaching them about Maslow's hierarchy. ✘
b ✔
c Maslow took the position that a person's competence is directly affected by the view they take of themselves. ✘
d ✔ **e** ✔
f The book on the topic was hers—I placed it on your desk. ✘

3 **a** Marisa's list of accomplishments helped her to build a sense of self-worth.
b Fiona and Charles's list of accomplishments included having a sense of humour.
c Friends who value you are important and a friend's acceptance is invaluable.
d Adolescents' feelings of belonging are affected when they try too hard to fit in.
e Once you see the child's self-image begin to improve, you will see significant gains in achievement.

f Adolescence causes stress on teenagers' bodies, minds and emotions.
g Emotional well-being is influenced by a person's ability to relate to other people.
h Self-esteem can be influenced by people's individual achievements.

4 In class today we discussed self-awareness. Everyone's feelings, behaviours and characteristics were discussed. We all agreed with Alyssa and Kieran's idea that people who are self-aware tend to make wiser decisions. The whole class's ideas were written on the board by Mr Pugh, while Yukiko typed up the notes on Than's laptop. He's been kind enough to let us use his laptop all term. We discussed how people's self-awareness may allow them to develop deeper relationships since they're more likely to understand what they want or need. Our class was really interesting.

UNIT 10 Virginia Woolf

Grammar pages 56–57

1 **a** F **b** S **c** S **d** F **e** F **f** S **g** S **h** F

2 **a** When **b** Although **c** Since **d** Because **e** While

3 **a** C **b** R **c** F **d** C **e** F **f** R

4 **a** ii **b** i **c** i **d** ii

5 (suggested answers)
a A moment later I saw the door open.
b Wanting the story to continue, she went on reading.
c Walking through the room, I saw a flashing movement that caught my eye.
d While I was at the door, I heard a sudden noise.
e Being a keen reader, I couldn't wait for the next novel to be released.

6 **a** A man and woman who occupy a house hear male and female ghosts. Wandering about the dwelling, they talk about finding a treasure.
b As love endures in *A Haunted House*, not even fate keeps the ghostly lovers separated and they exist in the afterlife together.
c Woolf reveals that connections are made between all souls, living and dead, and she examines these in great detail.
d The ghosts had occupied the house more than a century before the current residents, yet the living couple are unaware of them because they are asleep.
e After the man died, he joined his ghostly wife at the house they had once occupied and this was the same house where the living man and woman now reside.

7 **a** ✗ **b** ✓ **c** ✓ **d** ✗

Punctuation pages 59–60

1 **a** R **b** S **c** S **d** S **e** R **f** R

2 **a** Woolf was known for her mood swings. She also experienced bouts of deep depression.
b Two of Woolf's brothers had been educated at Cambridge but all the girls were taught at home and had access to the family's lavish Victorian library.
c The hormones of early adolescence spun Woolf into a nerthe parentvous breakdown and the death of her mother also deeply affected her.
d Her sister Vanessa and brother Adrian sold the family home in Hyde Park Gate. They then purchased a house in London.
e Woolf's novel *Mrs Dalloway* utilises interior monologues as a technique. It also highlights themes of feminism and mental illness in post-World War I England.

3 **a** Despite appearances, she continued to regularly suffer from bouts of depression[,] she suffered from dramatic mood swings as well.
b Long summer holidays were spent at Talland House in St Ives, Cornwall[,] this was considered a happy time for her.
c Stella, Virginia's sister, married Jack Hills in 1897[,] she too died suddenly on her return from her honeymoon.
d In 1921, Virginia's first collection of short stories appeared called *Monday or Tuesday* [,] most were written using a new style.
e Since about 1908, Virginia had been writing her first novel *The Voyage Out*[,] it was finished by 1913 but, owing to delays, it was not published until 1915.

4 (suggested answers)
a The effects of bipolar disorder at times caused Woolf to enter therapy and she withdrew from her busy social life. She was distressed that she could not focus long enough to read or write.

b She spent time in nursing homes for rest, she frankly referred to herself as 'mad', and she said she heard voices and had visions.

c Woolf wrote an extraordinary number of diaries, letters, critical reviews, essays, short stories and novels, which continue to be the source of much scholarly study. She is still popular today.

d Woolf's husband was watchful for the onset of the next depression in his wife. She would get migraine headaches and lie sleepless at night.

e Woolf's works examine the difficulties that female writers and intellectuals face and they are relevant today. Men are still perceived to hold uneven legal and economic power.

5 *A Room of One's Own* is an extended essay by Virginia [Woolf, it] **(C)** was first published in 1929. The essay was based on a series of lectures she delivered at two women's colleges at Cambridge University in England in [1928 the] **(R)** title of the essay comes from Woolf's perception that '... a woman must have money and a room of her own if she is to write fiction'. Woolf wrote that women have been kept from writing because of their relative [poverty, she] **(C)** believed that financial freedom would bring women the freedom to write. The title also refers to any author's right to [freedom] [Woolf] **(R)** strongly believed in an individual's right to be creative. The essay examines whether women are capable of producing work like [William Shakespeare it] **(R)** addresses the limitations women writers have faced historically and in the present.

Revision Test 2

Grammar pages 61–63

1 A tiny pebble got stuck in my shoe.

2 I am looking towards the future.

3 The food museum celebrates food and it celebrates cultural influence worldwide.

4 it

5 they

6 Since beginning to jog every evening, I feel a lot healthier.

7 I was about to answer the phone when it stopped ringing.

8 Before you arrived

9 that run on electricity

10 who woke up after 12 years

11 Within, in

12 After the theatre production

13 lunch

14 **(d)** The old lady who has lived next door for the last 20 years is very well known for the beautiful flowers in her garden.

15 The health reforms were implemented in all hospitals at the beginning of last year.

16 The effect of plastic trash on sea life is being investigated by Australian scientists.

17 Thinking about how literature has changed over time.

18 A new study finds that climate change has made winters a little bit warmer many bird species are now wintering a lot farther north.

19 In summer sunshine.

Punctuation pages 63–64

1 All four of them—Sinead, Seana, Isabel and Alex—decided to go cycling.

2 Hipparchus is known for the discovery of the first recorded nova (a new star).

3 Sustainability is about taking what we need to live now without jeopardising the future. We need to live in a sustainable way (this means something should be able to continue forever).

4 We are going overseas soon—I'm so excited—and I'm going to start blogging about it straight away.

5 A large proportion of all life, which mostly exists in the ocean, is unknown to this day.

6 Permaculture is a philosophy of working with nature, it relies on extended and thoughtful observation.

7 Permaculture is about growing your own food with green design. It works with people, our natural environment and ecosystems.

8 The delegate said, 'We believe every person should enjoy all of the rights stated in the Universal Declaration of Human Rights!'

9 'Amnesty International was founded after a group of students in Portugal were jailed for raising a toast to freedom', reported the student.

10 'Human rights', argued the lawyer, 'are the basic freedoms and protections that people are entitled to simply because they are human beings.'

11 What is it you're doing for your birthday this year?

12 Peta and James's school is going to have its first swimming carnival there.

13 I didn't want to be the one to show you Janay's house, but you would've found it anyway. It's next door to Fiona's place.

UNIT 11 Crime doesn't pay

Grammar pages 66–67

1
- **a** **i** are **ii** were
- **b** **i** is **ii** was, would
- **c** **ii** wanted
- **d** **ii** needed to take

2 **a** ii **b** i **c** i **d** ii **e** i **f** ii

3
- **a** The reporter asked how the museum would protect exhibits in the future.
- **b** The thief moaned that he had regretted this since it occurred.
- **c** The police officer said that they were extremely pleased to have located the dinosaur.
- **d** The thief admitted that he had been thinking of doing something like this for a while.
- **e** The museum manager exclaimed that they had never had anything like this happen before.

4
- **a** Police said, 'We have recovered a 1.6-metre-tall dinosaur that was stolen.'
- **b** The manager wondered, 'What has happened to the dinosaur during its absence?'
- **c** The manager said, 'I am exceptionally happy now.'
- **d** Dinosaur museum members said, 'We are relieved the dinosaur is back in its rightful place.'
- **e** The police asked the thief, 'Have you stolen anything else?'

5 **a** ii **b** i **c** ii **d** ii **e** i

Punctuation pages 68–69

1
- **a** 'Robbery is the crime of taking or attempting to take something of value by force, or threat of force, or by causing the victim to be fearful,' declared the police officer.
- **b** The lawyer explained, 'Robbery is different from other forms of theft, such as burglary, shoplifting or car theft, as it is violent in nature.'
- **c** 'Picking a victim's pocket is generally not considered robbery,' said Thomas, 'because there is no use of fear and because robbery requires more force than that necessary simply to remove the property.'
- **d** Wikipedia states, 'The most common situation is the hold-up, in which the robber threatens to shoot if valuables are not turned over.'
- **e** 'Robbery was one of the first crimes under English law to be made punishable by the government rather than through compensation,' explained the historian.

2
- **a** The word 'rob' evolved through French from Late Latin words of Germanic origin.
- **b** Highway robbery (or 'mugging') takes place outside or in a public place such as a footpath, street or car park.
- **c** Criminal slang for robbery includes 'blagging', 'stick-up' and 'steaming', the latter being organised robbery on underground train systems.
- **d** Robberies have been depicted, sometimes graphically, in various forms of media, and several robbers have become pop icons, such as George 'Baby Face' Nelson.
- **e** 'The Highwayman' by Alfred Noyes is a popular poem about an 18th-century robber.

3 **a** i **b** ii **c** ii **d** ii

4 **a** ✔ **b** ✘ **c** ✔ **d** ✘ **e** ✔

UNIT 12 Review of *The Sapphires*

Grammar pages 71–72

1

Low degree of certainty	Moderate/medium degree of certainty	High degree of certainty
might, sometimes, possibly, maybe, perhaps	should, ought to, would, often, could	is, will, cannot, absolutely, must, always, never

2 **a** could, possibly
b extremely, definitely
c certainty, is, could, always
d ought
e should, possibility, never

3 **a** couldn't **b** might **c** should **d** can't **e** must **f** might **g** should

4 **a** The film got a great response. The director must be thrilled.
b The girls are finally on their way to Vietnam. They must be very excited.
c Fiona's seen the film so talk to her. She should be able to tell you about it.
d He watches movies all night you know. That can't be healthy.
e I was thinking about what Kai said about the film. He may be right.
f I can't see the film listed on the noticeboard. It may have been cancelled.

5 **a** H **b** H **c** L **d** H **e** L

6 **a** 2 **b** 4 **c** 3 **d** 1

7 (suggested answers)
a In the film, the girls occasionally/sometimes let insensitive comments get them down.
b The original play has become a movie that may be interesting.
c It's possible that actor Chris O'Dowd may have reached an emotional peak in this role.
d The songs are rarely charming and enjoyable.
e You could possibly enjoy both the music and the performances.

Punctuation pages 74–75

1 **a** We are **b** It is **c** would have **d** that is, she is **e** will not, I will

2 **a** What's **b** I'll **c** she'd **d** Don't, you're **e** don't, can't

3 **a** I think Beyoncé's fantastic and I'm completely nowhere near where she is, but I aspire to be like her. I think she's amazing.
b Mauboy could've become the face of an alcohol brand but she believed it would've sent the wrong message to Indigenous communities.
c I've recently been home and spent some time with my dad. I miss that I can't see him more often and we're definitely going back soon. He'd really love that.
d It isn't too tricky—I've grown up singing and when I sing I'm proud. It's a great feeling.
e It was the most fun we've ever had in the studio and we couldn't have achieved it without everyone's support.

4 **a** At the age of 14, Mauboy's talents were exposed through the Telstra Road to Tamworth competition where she'd impressed everyone. **P C**
b Mauboy's now a member of the girl group Young Divas, replacing one of the group's original members. **C P**
c Mauboy's made several visits to Yipirinya School since the announcement that she's their official ambassador. **C C**
d We're pleased to announce that two dollars from every sale of Mauboy's nail polish was donated to Children's Hospital Foundations Australia. **C P P**
e Monday night's catch-up wasn't the first time Mauboy has come face to face with her idol. **P C**

5 Have you heard the new album? It's amazing. It's been played on most radio stations around Australia and it's bound to break domestic sales records. The album has such a cool look. Its cover is filled with images and colours and it's by far my favourite album of the year. It's definitely on my list of recommendations and its unique sound will certainly be popular.

6 Hi Jessica! We are huge fans of your music and can't wait to see your concert later this year. We think you're more than just a pop singer, and we really admire all the work you're doing with Australian youth. You're really turning into a fantastic actress as well! I've already ordered your new album and can't wait to listen to it.

7 I just spoke to Casey and Tiana and they're going to be at the concert too! I hope they bring their CDs to get signed. Have you been there before? It's my second time. The last time I nearly left my phone there. I was frantic with worry, but the concert organisers used their security guards to help me locate it. I think they're fantastic!

8 I've always loved singing although I didn't always know I would be successful. Fame's a difficult thing and I'm always trying to just be myself but it's hard. There's always something new to do and I've really enjoyed working with young Indigenous people. They'll say I'm a role model but for me it's also about being creative. It's about the music and the fans. I hope they'll listen and enjoy the music and remember all the great things they've got in their lives.

Grammar pages 77–79

1
- **a** Consequently—to show the result
- **b** however—to contrast ideas
- **c** Conversely—to contrast ideas
- **d** In conclusion—to conclude ideas
- **e** In addition—to add information

2 **a** furthermore **b** nevertheless **c** then **d** however **e** therefore

3
- **a** Raul explained how he changed his routine during one of his business phone calls. Instead of a conference call, he decided to switch to video because it allowed him to see his callers face to face.
- **b** Patricia found that the ability to communicate with her work colleagues using social networking and to be able to text them during conference calls and see them on skype has enabled her to feel connected.
- **c** Social media is surprising in that it fills a gap many workers feel when writing cold, impersonal emails as their primary source of communication.
- **d** The promise of the virtual workplace fails some people. They sometimes miss out on opportunities for it to improve their work experience.
- **e** Collaboration used to only occur between people in the same office. Today, it occurs between multiple people all over the world at the same time.

4 **a** ✗ **b** ✓ **c** ✗ **d** ✓ **e** ✗

5 **a** proper **b** method **c** At all times **d** discussion **e** appropriate

6 (suggested answers)
a burden/stress **b** eliminate
c associations/interactions/connections
d data/facts

7 All of these things are mostly positive and give you further opportunities for connecting with your friends. **2**

In conclusion, it is better to use a nickname as this is safer than providing your real name and it also makes it harder for people to identify you. **5**

Communication technologies such as mobile phones, email, blogs and social networking websites most likely play an important part in your social life. **1**

However, communication technologies can contribute towards unwanted attention and even unpleasantness. **3**

For example, once you put images or comments on a website or send them in an email, you have no further control over that material or how widely it is distributed. **4**

Punctuation pages 80–81

1
- **a** Technology has contributed to changes in our lives: we now talk less, stay indoors more and spend time creating online personas.
- **b** The parent's intentions were clear: no one would be using their devices during dinner.
- **c** My teacher demanded: 'Why are you using your phone during my lesson?'
- **d** Tamika created her invitation online. Only four classmates were invited: Lisa, Rolf, Hasheem and Maia.
- **e** Albert Einstein also said: 'The human spirit must prevail over technology.'

2
- **a** Plenty of students had contributed online to the class blog; Alyssa wanted to be one of them.
- **b** The most significant impact of technology on communication is the internet; for example, it allows us to send emails and chat.
- **c** Technology is amazing; however, it has contributed to loneliness for some who feel isolated.
- **d** Technology is no longer only a tool for survival; it has turned into a source of communication and entertainment.
- **e** Younger generations are participating in a massive, unintentional social experiment; the long-term effects of this are largely unknown.

3
- **a** Computers and the internet have eased the process of creating and editing documents. Think how often you use these tools: spell check, grammar check, cut and paste, and word count.
- **b** The internet has increased the speed of communication; consequently, the costs are reduced drastically.
- **c** The small keyboards on mobile phones make typing difficult and have resulted in a radical shortening of words; there is now little or no observance of traditional grammatical rules.
- **d** Communication has become concise and short: communication is now something achieved quickly and instantly.

e Technology has brought down the costs of communication significantly; as a result, it has improved people's access.

4 a ✗ b ✗ c ✗ d ✓ e ✓

5 There is increasing interest in how mobile phone use in schools influences student achievement; as a result, some school communities are calling for a complete ban of phones. This is an ongoing debate across the world: some schools are showing concern for the use of phones, while others are more certain the use of phones is of educational benefit. A representative from the Department of Education has stated: 'Phones should be discouraged unless they can be integrated into the learning program.' Some benefits of banning mobile phones in schools have been found to include the following: improved student achievement; higher concentration levels; and happier, more engaged students.

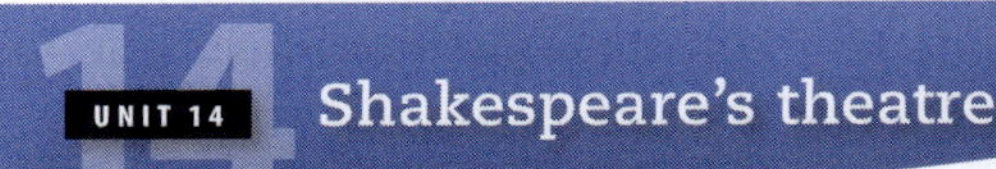

UNIT 14 Shakespeare's theatre

Grammar pages 83–85

1 a ii b i c ii d i e ii

2
- a The lamb is ready to eat its dinner.
- b It can be boring visiting neighbours.
- c The thief got 12 months in jail for stealing the guitar.
- d A car enthusiast who likes old cars visited the antiques showroom.
- e This is the photograph of my mother.

3 a ✓ b ✓ c ✗ d ✗ e ✓

4 (suggested answers)
- a Laughing hysterically, we thought the play was very funny.
- b Crossing the stage, the actor's costume fell down around his ankles.
- c While standing in line, we heard thunder boom loudly.
- d After singing on stage, the singer's performance received applause from the audience.
- e Totally destroyed by the fire, the theatre needed rebuilding.

5 a ii b i c ii d ii e ii

6
- a I'm absolutely certain the students decided to return again for a second time to the theatre.
- b Thanks to their joint collaboration, the university found the handwritten manuscript in the destroyed ruins of the writer's house, which was a great end result.
- c As an added bonus, the jokes were designed to hit their intended targets with precise precision.
- d They possibly might pack a lunch and bring along their own blanket for the outdoor performance.
- e The presence of the King at the performance was an unexpected surprise as he still remains popular.

7
- a ✓
- b The actor was asked to prepare quickly, thoroughly and accurately.
- c Shakespeare included characters who liked to fight, to eat and to dance.
- d The teacher said that he was a good reader because he paused at the right moments, used his voice with expression, and always looked up at the class.
- e The director told the actors that they should get a lot of sleep, that they should learn their lines, and that they should try to relax before the show.

Punctuation pages 86–87

1 a i/c b Inc. c Jnr, jr d kJ e km/h f accomm. g Dec. h assoc . i Dr j Prof. k mg

2 a does not equal b therefore c because d less than e degrees Celsius f approximately g decibel h feet/foot i at j without k any word ending in *ate*, e.g. L8 (late), L8ER (later)

3
- a United Nations
- b Very Important Person
- c Extra Terrestrial
- d Frequently Asked Questions
- e Random Access Memory
- f Liquid Crystal Display
- g Identification
- h World Health Organisation
- i Date of Birth
- j Australian Eastern Daylight Standard Time
- k Special Broadcasting Service
- l Master of Ceremonies
- m Member of Parliament/Military Police
- n Genetically Modified

4 (suggested answer)
Sh'peare born Stratford-upon-Avon, Warwickshire, UK 16th C. B/ween 1590 + 1613, he wrote approx. 37 plays /collab. on more →

great ach't. Many plays, e.g., *Macbeth* + *R&J*, espec. success. @ court and public p'houses. 1613, Sh'peare retired theatre + return. S-upon-A. Dcd + buried 1616.

5 The Bbc (BBC)*Television Shakespeare* is a series of British television (TV) adaptations of the plays of William Shakespeare. Transmitted in the U Kingdom (UK), the series spanned seven seasons and thirty-seven (37) episodes. By the end of its run, the series had proved both a TV ratings and financial success. 2Day (Today), the complete set is still a popular collection with ppl (people), and several eps (episodes) represent the only non-theatrical production currently available on Digital Versatile Disc (DVD). The series was shown in Aus (Australia) by the Aus Broadcasting Commission (abc) (ABC).

UNIT 15 Jasper Jones

Grammar pages 89–92

1 excellent, I think, I'm pleased, secret, creepy, fun, I believe, disappointing.

2
- **a** I thought he was trying to trick/fool me.
- **b** The job was easier to talk about than to complete.
- **c** The character was in trouble.
- **d** Are you fooling me/joking with me?
- **e** He might get fired/lose his job unless he starts getting to work on time.
- **f** She's turning into a lazy person, addicted to watching television.
- **g** I'm not sure that transaction was legal/permitted/allowed/authorised.

3
- **a** The character of Charlie Bucktin is as solid as a rock and everyone depends upon him in the novel.
- **b** Jasper Jones hopes to fly like an eagle; however, his circumstances do not support his independence.
- **c** Mr Wishart is on a steep learning curve and needs to toe the line or his family will be destroyed.
- **d** Charlie, although believing that every cloud has a silver lining, still needs to think outside the box to solve Jasper's problems.
- **e** Charlie hit the nail on the head with his solution to the problem and said it was a piece of cake.

4 (suggested answers)
- **a** The character was advised to improve his performance or else suffer the consequences.
- **b** Eliza is new and refreshing and she wants to support and care for Charlie.
- **c** As Mrs Wishart was feeling sick/tired/unwell, she was advised to rest.
- **d** Jasper was not out of trouble yet and needed to be vigilant/to monitor the situation.
- **e** The character needs to get back on schedule as there are people relying on him to take responsibility.

5
- **a** a story that has more than one level of meaning
- **b** the intended group of readers, listeners or viewers
- **c** the action of creating written, spoken or visual texts
- **d** factors that influence the creation of a text and its interpretation
- **e** an object used to represent something else
- **f** language that results in an emotional response
- **g** the categories that texts are grouped by, e.g . sci-fi, western, horror
- **h** the way information is arranged on a page or screen
- **i** a fictional story of events and experiences
- **j** giving human qualities to things, animals and emotions

6
a argument **b** independence
c government **d** continuation
e nominalisation **f** advancement
g persistence **h** inspiration
i introduction **j** promotion **k** reflection

7
- **a** The author depicts Corrigan realistically and accurately.
- **b** Due to the writing style, the reader becomes involved in the novel.
- **c** Charlie and Jeffrey relate to each other in a friendly way, as shown by humour.
- **d** The way characters' lives are described creates interest for the reader.

8
- **a** Charles Bucktin is intellectual rather than athletic/energetic.
- **b** Charles desires/wishes to become a writer, and reads significant/essential books during the course of the novel.
- **c** Charlie thinks that Jasper looks significantly/considerably older.
- **d** Jasper has a poor/negative/undesirable reputation, but often is blamed for crimes he does not commit.

- **e** Eliza, Charlie's girlfriend, is described as clever/shrewd/intelligent and has the appearance of Audrey Hepburn.
- **f** As a result/By reason/In consideration of his Vietnamese heritage/culture, Jeffrey often experiences racial discrimination. However/Nevertheless, he accepts the abuse/mishandling/cruelty with good humour.

Punctuation pages 93–94

1

- **a** Jasper is forced to hide from Corrigan; otherwise, he may be targeted by the police.
- **b** Charlie does not reject Jasper's request for help; instead, he chooses to follow him.
- **c** Eliza, meanwhile, waits for Charlie at the bookshop as they had planned.
- **d** Charlie is exhausted; nonetheless, he waits patiently to see if Jasper will arrive.
- **e** Consequently, the events cast a shroud of fear over the little town of Corrigan.

2

- **a** Charlie's mother, Ruth, promotes her image as a good mother, wife, member of the CWA and civic volunteer. She is a demanding, and at times difficult, mother and she and Charlie appear to have an uneasy relationship. However, he does seem to get on with his father very well.
- **b** When Charlie finds his mother in a relationship with a man who is not his father, the power balance shifts between them. When this happens, Ruth loses her control over Charlie, and Charlie learns to redefine his attitudes towards his mother.
- **c** Pete Wishart, Laura and Eliza's father, is the most aggressive character in the novel. Although he appears to be a man of moral standing, the audience learns he is quite the opposite.
- **d** In spite of their own wicked, depraved, and corrupt behaviour, Corrigan's citizens have decided that Jasper Jones is a bad influence. He is often accused of committing a crime, despite his protestations, even when he was nowhere near the event when it occurred.
- **e** Even though he is a thief, Jasper behaves with honour and integrity. Although he is a boy, not yet an adult, he feels he failed to protect Laura. Charlie tries to uncover what she needed protection from, but Jasper keeps her secrets even after she's gone.

3

Yes, I was there. It was horrific, actually. After Jasper got her down, I fell into a stupor of disbelief and couldn't believe it was happening. Life's pretty funny, isn't it? One day you're coasting along, nothing really unusual happens, and then you get the fright of your life. This will really change who I am, I suppose. I wish I'd never met Jasper Jones, left my house or gotten involved, you know.

4

- **a** Like Jasper, Jeffrey Lu's family is also unwanted and unwelcome.
- **b** Australian men, including those who are from Corrigan, are drafted to fight in the Vietnam War.
- **c** The Lus, despite being residents of Corrigan, are exposed to ongoing racism and abuse.
- **d** The Lus try hard to show their allegiance to Australia, but their attempts are met with contempt.
- **e** Jeffrey is called 'Cong' by the cricket team, a reference to the Viet Cong, and his heritage is mocked.

5

Jasper Jones begins as Charlie Bucktin is approached by Jasper Jones, the town trouble-maker, who claims to have discovered his girlfriend, Laura, in a tragic position. Jasper, who believes that he will be blamed, asks Charlie to promise him not to tell anyone what happened. Although he immediately feels worried, Charlie agrees, but wants to tell the police. Charlie is terrified, however, that the police already know of his involvement.

The novel, as it unfolds, touches on many social, moral, personal and emotional issues. From a dramatic opening chapter, as seen through the eyes of Charlie Bucktin, it exposes the life of a country town, and reveals its hidden and shady secrets.

Charlie develops, over a period of several months, from an innocent 13-year-old, and sees more of life and its dark side than he really should. The book, nonetheless, is not all serious. The exchanges between Jeffrey Lu, his best mate and a Vietnamese Australian, are at times enormously amusing. Even during serious moments, Charlie is able to produce a smile from the reader through his honest observations.

The main interaction occurs between Charlie and Jasper Jones, a young loner, who is ostracised by the people of Corrigan, and branded as the local trouble-maker. These two, who are bound together by circumstance, form a deep bond that will establish their friendship for life.

Revision Test 3

Grammar pages 95–97

1. The student complained that he always got chosen first for public speaking.
2. The boy said, 'I've eaten the whole cake after all!'
3. I think it could perhaps influence the committee's decision.
4. must
5. However
6. it
7. beneficial
8. produced
9. The owners told the employees that they would receive a pay rise.
10. After reading a fantastic book, the movie based on it is guaranteed to be thrilling.
11. Hoping to excuse my lateness, the note explained that I had been ill overnight.
12. free
13. unconfirmed
14. together
15. They described swimming at the beach, climbing local hills, and having lunch at the local restaurant.
16. Tran liked to watch movies, share stories with his friends, and read a book before bedtime.
17. I don't like it when the character decides to leave home.
18. I was moved to tears when the old lady was reunited with her child.
19. Let's listen to some old records today during lunch.
20. The character really burns the midnight oil in her attempt to seek revenge.
21. The student recounted what happened during her school trip to Tibet.
22. representation
23. concluded

Punctuation pages 97–99

1. The teacher said, 'This student's essay is very well structured.'
2. The politician explained that they wanted to end the burden of debt for students.
3. Delilah
4. It's been so wonderful to see her writing develop.
5. theirs
6. The teacher would've handed back their essays but there wasn't time.
7. The school's rules were clear: no one would have access to their devices during the day.
8. While visiting Vienna in 1781, Mozart was dismissed from his Salzburg position; he chose to stay in the capital, where he achieved fame but little financial security.
9. A delegate from the UN is a VIP, although they do require ID in order to verify themselves.
10. Gov.
11. Author Tim Winton was born in Karrinyup, Western Australia, but moved at age of 12 to Albany.
12. Winton has lived in Italy, France, Ireland and Greece, but he currently lives in Fremantle, near Perth, with his wife and three children.
13. While at university, Winton wrote his first novel, *An Open Swimmer*, which won The Vogel Literary Award in 1981, launching his writing career.
14. It wasn't until *Cloudstreet* was published in 1991, however, that his writing career was properly established.
15. His novel *Breath* was published in 2008. His latest novel is *Eyrie*, published in 2013.